i

c

o

p

e

YOU AND OTHER PIECES

COREY ZELLER

"this we were, this is how we tried to love,
and these are the forces they had ranged against us,
and these are the forces we had ranged within us,
within us and against us, against us and within us."
—Adrienne Rich

CONTENTS

Farm

My Morning Song is Better than Yours

The House is a Place Where Things Can Go Wrong

You and Other Pieces

FARM

FARM

The green shot of the earth. The coffee in squares of ice. The walled. The shed in the back completely covered in ivy. A rocking chair painted twenty times in fifty years. An arm missing. Your thank you, which sounds nothing like that. Something you said by her small aquarium that day. All that blue rock of the bottom. The gray shape against the glass. A gill spilled open.

A first wound. Logs of split wood under new snow. A toy phone you bought the baby girl. The eyes that bobbed up and down when you pulled the cord across the wood floors. A fake ring. Up and down and the shrubbery outside roped for the winter. A door off its hinges, leaned against the house. And what was that story?

A refrigerator fell down your uncle's steps. His coat covered with grain. And you liked holding that coat in your lap didn't you? Like another badly-drawn villain the anvil got the better of. Balanced on his pinky finger, his nose. And somehow the rocking chair moved out there in the wind. Leaves tumbled below it.

And the wool your uncle shaved from the lambs. The electric lights extension-corded about the rafters. The tufts of white noise covering the mud. How we'd volunteer ourselves to help with the work. Those mornings, so cold you could pour coffee from your thermos into a tray, put it into cubes for the baby girl to suck.

And even back then we knew borders went further than all those acres. The town just a series of things. And you kept repeating north to me in the dark, below the red quilt you made in high school.

NORTH:
In full, the speech of try, of free, of quoting old thinkers and realizing they were wrong.

NORTH:
How every time the storms came, pieces of roof were in the grass. We wanted to be anyone but the middle, but all this gray came in pieces. Like a ferry of clouds, a clot, a birdbath anything but a birdbath. Even the finches gone, the sheets soaked.

And you were teaching me to live my life as a joke inside a joke. The populations of you seemed endless and unbroken and I couldn't decide if your mouth was a chalice or a padlock. The snow below us crushed like aspirin. You tossed feed to the air from a barrel the way a movie cowboy tries to blind the black hat who got the jump on him. And the dark chickens went on clawing and ducking. You made some kind of moo song.

You got sick on bad milk from a bucket, wore that flannel scarf through all the fevers that came. Around your neck like a noose. As if wrung to the ceiling and sky. And it was funny when you put it over your mouth like you'd been kidnapped in a movie, but I hated it over your eyes. A firing squad was coming. A luxury of bullets, the detailed ripping of smoke and red, and you, finally still.

Still as the knife on the counter there still. Those mothballs in a chest. The chest with clear bags and newspaper clippings and your scarf inside it. The baby girl could put a mothball in her mouth and suck it. The way too close to a light bulb burns. A jar you kept pencils and markers inside. And even a doorknob of a lion, from wherever doorknobs of lions come from. The tips of shoes all pressed into corners.

And outside there was blue and stars and sun in the sky all at once and I held a bit of rusted gate in my hand and you touched my coat, brand new, touched my coat like a crystal ball and told me that the future was made of down.

And North became northeast. Astray. And it began.

What was over-simple made graves in us. The geese pulled away from each other and the geese pulled apart, pulled apart. I saw feathers and huge, blue, industrial buckets full of legs, twigs and red. Someone's keys were jangling from their belt. And the rubbing of wet gloves. A ceremony of hands and birds and all direction this direction. Whatever the opposite of flight is. The way an ancient inventor must have taken apart a wooden flying machine. A design he based on his study of birds. A study that concluded with the knowledge he was not them, that his hands would never brush against the utmost tips of the trees, the highest of green.

And how many tries had he made? And how long? And what misjudgment had he made in the incline? In the wind? And I suppose he must have been a little like us, doing any odd job no matter how foul. Watching the sky tip over into ground. Knowing the insides of a wing. It's true working, how wind is always exiting its bottom, never holding it, tucking it away. How flying is working against the wind. The way a man tries to find the top of a lake as not to drown. The lake.

The reflection of the geese in the water so much like the hesitation of your cool, unmeaning hand moving closer, closer, blasting through bedrock. And I'm steadily rubbing my blue jeans. Worn with two long weeks of work. And I'm rubbing to stay warm. That's what I say, at least. And I taste plastic. I feel blue being stripped from my eyes.

UNFELT:

A Northern song. The way one mistakes a bridge with a headache, with a pure and manic pattern of notes, with sugar spilled on the floor.

A record in your room left spinning on its table, the static sound and the baby girl barking at herself in the mirror, the vibrations of her mouth. And you just left it playing there like that. I put my thumb over your face in a picture on the dresser and the sex of the no-head picture seemed uncertain like the time we took the screens out of all the windows for uncle. You behind one. All those little pins of light. Their absurd slur and fall through black mesh, and you.

Already Northbound and almost threadbare, a circle of light beyond a circle of dark. And I remember that old car we found at the abandoned airfield just outside of town, the one full of leaves. I remember you kept things in the trunk, things wrapped in white paper. And I was never sure if it was the moon or the moon glow that burned. All I knew was that the dead engine of that strange machine was a confessor. An apostle who taught us that everything stops. Stops literally at the exact spot of liftoff. A machine trying to do what it isn't capable of doing. A failed, mad inventor in a series of mad inventors.

Trying. Those nights out there with trees in collective, the empty runway useless, starting to cover with grass. And the old shell of a car someone had left behind. They must have seen something. And maybe they left me a clue. Maybe they took off, got somewhere. I doubt it, but maybe. But for sure, I knew, they'd been trying. Failure after failure, invention after invention, test after test.

ROAD

You hear static in the baby monitor sky. You hear crying.
The white flakes shred off it. The New Year's Eve song.
The people you've forgotten. Everywhere. Cities, states,
whole maps of missing people. On milk cartons. You've
been sleeping on people's porches, in unlocked cars, but
now the weather has changed. You've stained your favor-
ite shirt with red wine but you wear it almost every day.
Your shirt is part of the scenery. You're part of the piles
of clothes.

This is the third time Paul the Trucker has found you.
The world is big. So big. Yet here you are on the road
with Paul again. He has a bed for you to sleep on behind
the front seats. Box upon box of coconut cupcakes that
rot the teeth up into your blood. Your enamel soaking
into you the way socks full of pennies in juvenile halls
did. He talks in dim devices. His glasses shine a kind of
blue light from all the passing machines. A whistle comes
from where a tooth was. He grins too much. His boxed
face. His face a baby's head on a grown man. His bread-
basket mouth.

You're missing food stamps now, with these blue lines on
old routes that lead nowhere. A nowhere that screams
like a horror movie in a theatre slept-in. You kept waking.

You saw a wolf man running through woods. Howling. Saw fog that was enough to take a man in forever and never let go. Fog that would take you in, suck you though a giant, fast-food straw. And you hear Paul's tongue clacking, an oil drill. Bringing up black from the deepest. You hear it smash into a purr. As immediate as a novelty postcard. His dispenser mouth.

Split. A dumb-wild seed of God. This is what Paul tells you. That there is scripture sown into the Earth, crosses to pass. Billboards we pass. There is scripture there. Heartburn where the color of a dress you'd once seen finds you. Shaking. It fills you the way the end of a broomstick fills you. Whiter than any room you've ever seen. Your cheeks flush. Your forgetting cheek. The cold hand against it. The blind hands which are running their palms on the white walls inside you. Fills you: a child riding alone on an airplane for the first time. To see his mother. His father. After a long time. And all the stewardesses are so, so kind. So kind.

Now Paul tells you about God. He says God is a warm house. Is something terrible a surgeon cuts out of you. God is back. Is getting back to something. A block you once lived on one terribly happy summer of thick hanging trees. Is the sound of someone talking in the next room. Older people. People who know better. People like God. Which really doesn't matter where me and Paul are now. We're sparrow-humbled. We're that hippy girl I knew singing an old jazz song to me the night she learned she was going to die. She said see. See. While the asthma of the lawns made a wheeze sound from her window.

The yellowed porcelain of the morning sky heeled into us and I think now of something I read. Women whose feet have been ruined by shoes. Shoes. Can you believe it? Human parts ruined by such tiny things. Can you believe it? Shoes.

I do. Paul does also.

He's talking about God again. He's talking about God in a way I didn't even know talking could do.

He says God is the interstate's broken ankle. Twig-thin. The gray, alligator skin of the road below us enormous, informative. Because the interstate says just as God says. In the cough syrup taste of afternoons and the jungle of black wires above us. We wait. We count Mississippi after Mississippi. Still the road says as God says. Says breakage, doubt, and birch smell. Says like droning mosquitoes from your old life of yellow. Says atlas, embroidery. Says the pines look as white and sad as a Japanese clown. Says your eyelids are paper fans. The crumpled blinking. Blinking. That engine of blinking combusting into wordless articles. The articles of your life. Like a razor against old newspaper. Cutting away and saving the white space, the borders. Just color from the funnies without the funny. Just color.

Just the interstate swallowing the truck and Paul and I whole in the snow. Into the mouth of God. God's mouth which is a carnival tunnel of love some mechanical swan is floating on. Because after all the green water and fake hearts there is kissing. No one tells you that. That there's kissing in the dark tunnel. When the dark happens and no one can see. There's kissing in the dark of God's mouth. It's a secret. Don't tell. Two bodies wrestling inside a mechanic swan. A double-hearted machine.

Sun-hurt. It pulls a sound from you like someone tugging a gold necklace from your throat. That cool strain and run of it against your tongue. Paul cursing the drivers. Because the road here is different than in a town. Anything can happen. Even with the gold that spills from you. Anything can be taken away. Suspicion measured in the length of a fire. From long to short. The evidence of fire is substantial. Holds weight. Fire to fire you grow like mythology. A God. Your body somehow staying upright. Like an old barn you once saw. An old barn whose whole frame relied upon the strength of a single nail.

We stray. We're guided by raw material. Or maybe it's just movement. The incompletion of every action, every gesture. Or the loneliness of a standstill. Paul moves because he has nothing but the back of this gray alligator. He's a swamp man. His heart is fine china. He must want to have some kind of tea party with God when eternity comes. Because he is shining his insides clean with dust. The brightest dust you can imagine. So bright it hurts your eyes like teeth gleaming in movies. Like leaving those movies in the middle of the afternoon after a long nap. Attic dust. A piñata of unused things. Bust me open, he says. But do it with your eyes closed.

Peel. The skin of the eyes like a patio of well-dressed people who are holding scissors to the sky. Cutting at air.

Men and women cutting at the shell of the sky and getting nothing. People with money to burn. Literally. Inside the hollowed face of a statue. A gasmask kissing a gasmask.

Because God is like getting instructions on your first day of work. The cathedral of a young nipple. A blue jay or a cardinal in the snow. Make it twenty cardinals in the snow. A hundred cardinals in the snow. Because God is like that. A body thrown from a high bridge. The arms torn from a clock. Swallowed fire. The way day is no longer day. Is fathers gathered to cry alone, together, long away from their families in a desert that other deserts are afraid of. Is their memorial of beer bottles. Is wallowed God.

Paul is talking. I learn talking from Paul. The way a dead man asks for his grave to be dug. But only for digging. Only for digging and digging till the diggers forget to bury him. This is our lesson on talking. On eternity. Eternity which is like the snow asking for the warmth of the sun. Is the slow strip of a woman in a closet. Or what might as well be a closet. Is livid no. Is the profanity of the street wooing you out of the dark. Out of your bed. Is the reign of distant towns and the leather they strap into your teeth and shudder you lonely like a madman playing a piano with his hands clenched into fists. Like the callous shell of a lobster a poor couple didn't know how to eat. Who later go to their hotel. Laughing about not knowing how to eat a lobster. Laughing. A kind of laugh like every person you never had to know but did. You knew them. Knew them like the sound of someone moving furniture around the apartment above you. Simply through movement. Whole lives lived in movement and elsewhere.

How a woman is getting her hair ready while her husband mows the lawn. This is a story that passes when you pass through a town. Nothing special. Maybe a first kiss. Maybe the first inclining to a kind of violence. A violence not known. Very little. Very little happens when you pass through a town but passing. But maybe in that house, on that corner, a woman is taking blue curlers from her hair. Is getting ready to make love to her husband in the same room they always make love. If they call it that. Love. Like the blue plastic that covers shirt after shirt waiting to be picked-up at a dry cleaners. Rows of blue plastic and blue walls. A place that hadn't changed since the sixties. This is what happens to love. This hooking. This covering. So clean and precise.

Paul comes to a halt at a truck stop somewhere between an itch and an uppercut. He hates the others and the methamphetamines. The cringe readied. He sees them drinking and popping pills with hookers beside a long row of trucks and sees also the impassable shadow of God. I've seen them too. Seen so much out there. But prefer this version. This version of Paul and I. Paul and I and his talk of God. So this is the version I tell. Because everyone has their own version of the road and what it was like out there. How it ended. With some it ended like youth. With others a release. A long sentence served that ended in a lifetime of parole they never lived down. Because they knew, all along, there were others still locked there. And they carry them wherever they go. The way the readied grind their teeth into mush.

So you go on. With your paper plate sadness. With the awkward shape of you. With cut hair. You go on. You find God. He's a spy in a soup kitchen drinking light from a Styrofoam cup. He's with dreads, smoking. He's blue eyes. The sort of blue that makes people stare for a long time. Like heat lightning. Like children looking out windows when they're not allowed to go outside. Like where a stolen bicycle was. Just the night before. Like walking across the lake one winter. Across an entire lake for the first time and you go home and tell your uncle. You tell him you walked across a whole lake on your own feet like a polar bear cub and he beats the awe right out of you. Not with his belt. Your aunt's. A thick, purple lashing. Like snow blowing back into the sky. Like a skinned polar bear walking up stair after stair. And stair after stair you lose another polar bear part. Because God is a story about staircases. He is a staircase which doesn't lead to a door, or a balcony, or anything else. He leads to light. Not a light like you're thinking. Like immaculate or pure or like you'd read in the Bible. Just a light that clears when you reach it. Clears like a lens focusing on a subject. Maybe the wrong one. But that's between you and God. God who's a corpse at an all-black funeral you stumbled into looking for coffee. To bum a cigarette. All these black guys in fresh suits looking at you and knowing what you were doing. So you cried. You cried because you were the earth's one bad tattoo. The only one it was ashamed of.

How Paul used to say that he wanted his happiness to grow eyes. To grow eyes and a mouth and a body. He wanted his happiness to be a body living a life somewhere just so when he was sad he would know it was alive. Somewhere. And a part of it was a part of him. From him. Like a child.

LOT

To crane information. To calculate every cereal bowl and dead headlight. To fret over an old registration sticker. A top to something. Thirty bucks you'd borrowed from a guy named Wop. Call me Wop, he said. You collected cans for him. Got bit by a white dog collecting cans from him. A white dog that had followed you almost three blocks. Call me Wop, he said. You smelled of white mutt. You smelled of mud in pale fur. In clumps and clumps of eggshell-colored mane. Now the DJ on the radio is telling you that the mountains here were originally at the bottom of the ocean. How they knew this because of fossils. Fossils of prehistoric octopuses they'd found at the top of the mountain. How the earth shifts the way your girlfriend's feet would scrunch your blanket all the way to end of the bed. Because the earth moves this way. It is the scrunching of a blanket, pulled sheets.

It is the unremarkable drag race coursing through you. A game of chicken. Two cars pointed at each other with their engines revving and coughing and slurring and stuttering car noises at each other. Or the wedding veil that hid the bloated face of a boy playing on a sidewalk, white as the froth soon spilling from your mouth. A veil. A stick he was running through an anthill. Under your skin. Your skin the color of a TV show even your aunt and uncle are too young to remember. Where people call a boy "son" and mother "mother" and father "father" and so on.

How you've been living in the lot. Bathing in the pond out back in the woods. Listening to the radio in the car you'd hidden below cut branches. The last human animal. How you touch the boarded windows of the abandoned mall in the lot when you're dizzy. You touch boarded windows and cry and vomit and yell with all the lonesome of the world. And you're doing it again. You can never tell a story straight. The dog. It had put something in you. Your left hand isn't working. Muscles clenching and twitching. Something is inside. You know its name but can't say it. Just know it. Feel it in your craw-fish mouth. Feel it scurry and snap it's pinchers at your reflection in the rearview mirror. In the irregular light. How the light seems to be picking out the black sediments of air. The preservation of fences inside you. With silver rot. How your girlfriend's mouth once tasted of mint as wine spilled on a checkered floor. Her silver lipstick. What the body obeyed. A flash of invisible insects forging and humming through the orange-yellow dawn of barbwire trees. All knuckle and steel against your shoulders in the grass-choked dusk.

And you know the gas tank is empty but you try the engine anyway. You think of driving to a hospital. To surgical masks who take you in and fix you with calm precision. You whirl over the crumbling posters of kids wearing glasses on the side of the empty mall. An old eyeglass store. They're smiling at you and you're wearing a pair of old frames you'd found in a box. The lenses just clear plastic. But you loved how the wire frames made you look smarter. Older. The person you were supposed to become.

You think of this and it makes you sick. You think you should eat. You get a can of baked beans from the trunk and eat it without cooking it. You seesaw with nausea. With every gulp. You hang out the car door and scout the brush beyond the concrete for wood to make a fire. You feel the divide between you and the earth. The lot. How it hangs there ready to swallow you whole. Un-returning. With battery eyes. With the spoons you stole from an unlocked house. The brief spurts of their clattering when you drove through the mountains. Tiny, festering guillotines. The root of silverware's public sounds pining away into plates in roadside diners where an old man with gold hair transplants is fiddling with the keys of a glowing jukebox. A coil of vinyl crowned inside it. With the hacking of screen doors. With one leg on every table always a little too small and wobbling. How a waitress with a hearing aid and a wire hanging from her ear tells you it's bad luck to bring an open umbrella inside.

How you'd sleep beside the highway sometimes before the lot. You'd wake to sirens or noon singeing your eye-brows. How your aunt had forgotten she'd turned the gas on the grill and when your uncle pushed the button it burned his eyebrows clean off. How he ran to the side of the house and let the hose run over his head for a long time. With his eyes closed, there, he was a statue in a fountain. Your days always begin that way. You hear this voice. This voice that's familiar but they swear they have the wrong number and you're too much of a coward to ask again. Or your days begin running, deeper and deeper, a kid in a field with your baseball mitt in the air but the ball never comes down and you end up just crashing into a fence. Just how you find yourself in the lot. Hanging from a fence and forgetting how you got there. Shouting at the lines on the concrete. How you suddenly realize you're the joke worn thin. You're a bomb threat at your old school when the older kids always had to take the younger kids outside by the hand and nothing happened. Just the same windows. The same doors.

But you've finally got a fire burning in the lot. It makes the fake lenses of your glasses fog. You pace around the handicap signs feeling as ordinary and vivid as anything else in the reinvented world. You watch the leaves turn in the air. How your aunt used to sit in her favorite chair with a book in her lap. Peeling pages back the same way she pet the dog. For hours. Till she put a distinct crease in the corner of every book. But it didn't matter. The bent books. One day the rain came in from an open window and ruined them all. You remember the afternoon she'd thrown them away. You were playing on the porch with the dog and she came back on the porch in nothing but her bra. She was holding her soaked shirt and saying she was tired. So tired. She sat on the stoop and promised she'd sew your shirt in the morning. She said this and then told you a secret. She told you that bees, all bees, can distinctly remember human faces. She told you this and sometime later you went to the hornet's nest in the shed out back and tried jumping up to the hole in it. So the bees could see you.

Then all the bandages and the oils and the fresh hyacinths she'd cut for you. Her kiss goodnight and good morning on your welted cheek. A kind of Elephant Man. But your life of carnival acts and caravans never happened. You healed instead. You healed and you learned that your aunt would always lean forward when she talked about things she wanted for her life and back when she spoke of her time before you. She spoke warmly when she drank something cold and sadly when she drank something hot. You learned there was nothing sadder than a cup of coffee in your aunt's hand.

But you're a long way from that and anything else.

You feel the sickness the dog put in you growing. Foam forms around the mouth.

The fire in the lot fades on its own when the wind picks up. Embers scatter across the lot and North toward the shape of the mountains you can still somewhat see in the dark.

You hear nothing but wind.

Wind.

You go back to the car and wrap yourself in a blanket. Just you and the small bits of ember still burning and floating up and up and up and up in the darkness of your skull. Over and over. Ember and the whizzing of air against the windows of the car. The creaking of tree limbs and aluminum. Grass split by the wind ghosting itself across the land.

HOSPITAL

Balloon. You watch the balding girl bounce it up in the air behind the blue-gray windows of the doctor's station. Up, down, and never listening to the doctor. The doctor who is standing. Solemnly. Patiently. Professionally. He's trying to tell her something. Something important. With her reddened face. With the few stands of black hair left on her head. Her blotched and reddened and with plasma collected. Radiated. How superheroes get their powers in comic books. Burns but without powers. Without the bubbles of conversation floating above her head. Without Mr. Fantastic's arms stretching her out further and further from what the doctor is saying. Arms that keep going and wrap her in elastic cradle above the skyline. To a park somewhere she could bounce her balloon. Not just the exhale of the plain buildings outside. All the weather-less hours of her life. Veins and charts and tests and x-rays and laughing. How she still thinks it's funny when she sees her skeleton. Laughs. With the Indian burn of her gown brushing the scars on her now flat chest.

How you're waiting with a kind of weirdness running through you because you feel a damp contraction in the bed you're standing beside. A half-living infant. Trying to be born out of itself. But still as a bird that's hit a window.

The white owl that smashed into the kitchen window of your aunt's house and broke its neck. Still. Completely still. But moving somehow. How having a body gives you a very small feeling. A tiny feeling. Your body: a box full of fake jewelry. Your body: those small, paper hearts the kids in the ward made. How you're helping the nurse take them down from the walls. Dozens of them. How you put a few in your pocket. Hearts. The ones with names.

You put them in your pocket with the four-cornered picture Jenna gave you to look at when you needed to remember how far you'd come. How the first corner is just your one eye, the side of your whitened mouth, and the haircut a nurse gave you. Slicked-back with a black comb. "You're a greaser," Jenna said. And you find it hard to look at. Even harder than the second fold of the picture. The second fold being your face foaming. In the third, you see your arms in restraints. Tensed. Bruce Banner turning into the Hulk. Only you weren't shattering helicopters with your fists and flattening bullets with your teeth. You were terrified of something as small as water. A glass on a tray would make you go blood-curdled. Worse than how they tried to shave you then and got tiny cuts on your face. Worse.

Back then, days went by the same way you used to shift around public ashtrays looking for halves of cigarettes, clattering, a coat hanger clattering in a half-open closet. With your life in halves, in folds. Your life a pocket. A pocket of mountains beyond the hospital that hide the crash test dummying of clouds. Clouds stacking themselves the way cars stack on huge spikes below the interstate. How something is always gathering where you're not. Will never be. With your neurosis of water and melting snow. Fake snow. Snow. With the missed, slept-through shifts of your life. With your life an action figure never taken out of plastic. Your life an unused, unworn collectible.

How you're waiting for Jenna now. Waiting for her to come with her camera and the dried cranberries she'll probably have put in a bag for you. With the big green coat she got when she was photographing the winter Olympics decades ago. The one she always wears. Always wears because she's too cheap to turn the heat on in our apartment. The apartment she lets me sleep in for free. In blanket after blanket cause it's always cold enough to see the air steaming out of your mouth like dried ice. How you watch her work in the darkroom in her green coat and think of the ice skaters she'd taken pictures of. Their complete and certain friction. The crystalline structure. The axels and rotations. How skating makes you think of a long time ago. People in old-fashioned clothing skating on a pond below a covered bridge. How Jenna is taking pictures of people in the hospital for the doctor's records. For insurance companies. How someday they will look old. They will look less hurt and more unreal. What ghosts are supposed to be.

Code R. That's what Jenna said on the phone. You'd be taking pictures of a Code R. And you have to go. You have to go because Jenna is teaching you a craft. A skill. Because doing odd jobs around the hospital isn't enough to pay all the medical bills. Being the doctor's mascot. A pathetic bobcat in a tee-shirt at a football game. "That's no way to live," Jenna says. So you watch her take pictures. With your head nodding and fetching this and that. How you never truly notice the people you're taking pictures of until you develop them with Jenna. Like that baby who was born dead. That baby who had another baby head blooming from its neck. A mutant. An X-Man. Two heads tied to the same stillborn life. Or the roofer who fell from a house in the rain. How his nail gun somehow shot nails all over him on the way down. How the picture shows him with a few nails sticking out of his head and arm. And he was saying he was lucky. That the rain had made the ground soft enough to break his fall. Because the body is not Colossus with his indestructible skin. Because the body is subject to the world. The world. Like Magneto pulling the metal off of Wolverine's bones. How that comic made you wonder how it hadn't happened sooner. How it was right there. So easy. All the time.

You eventually find Jenna in her green coat and waiting by an office with a policeman and a doctor. They've brought a girl in. Younger than usual. And you listen without making yourself known. Because you dread what's coming. Her bruises. The picture's Jenna will take of her privates. All those pictures of women's privates in Jenna's apartment. Because Code R is always the worst. The women with their sobbing. Their humiliation. Their different and many colors of hair. How the cops ask them question after question about who'd done it to them. With someone making sketches and the woman crying. Telling them about the shape of his nose. His

eyes. His skin. Every inch of him. They make her re-
member. Sketch him. A comic book artist sitting around
trying to come up with a new villain. One worse than
ever before. Sketch after sketch. With the police asking.
Over and over. "What happened?"

But somehow this girl is different. You feel the herding
sound of many and various animals trampling inside her.
Animals running from some invisible storm. Running on
pure instinct. With that locomotive push of many things
moving inside the wild where no one goes. Inside her.
Where no one is allowed. You feel trampling and a sad-
ness only a child knows. That song Jenna's Yugoslavian
grandmother sang at her son's birthday party. How that
song must have been famous a long, long time ago but
no one knew it. Remembered it. No one listened. Just sat
around drinking while little boys in cowboy outfits took
shots at each other again and again. Pretending to die.
In slow-motion. In exaggerated gurgles of translucent
blood only they could see. Pouring from them. Holding
the holes that weren't really inside them. Holding them
to keep their fake, cowboy blood from pouring all over
the floor, human watering cans. Boom-boom. And they
pointed their fingers at each other. At you. At mirrors.
How you pointed Jenna's camera into a mirror at your-
self and took a picture. But when you turned the camera
around to look at yourself you only saw the white, hot
light of the flash. Whitened over your chest as if you were
a saint, a superhero holding a glowing orb of powerful
energy. Holding it like those matted leaves your cousins
threw over you as a kid. Taunting you. Burying you below
all that wet and color and dead, earthy smell. Your cous-

ins who shot fingers at each other too. With you rising out of a huge pile of leaves, a monster, a Frankenstein. In the woods. With autumn wheezing inside your chest. Wheezing: the shutter-closing sound of Jenna's camera. Chick-chick. And time stops. Mr. Freeze shot ice all over everything and stuck it there. Stopped it precisely under a thick coat of ice. Because that's what photography is. You decide what to document. How to document it. You shift life into frames. You decide. How Jenna spread some on the floor and glued others to the wall one afternoon. Drawing lines from one picture to another. Right on the wall. In chronology. "False," you said to her. You said it looking at a blurred picture she'd drained the color from. "False." A dream you once told someone, a lie. But you had to lie. To explain how you felt in a way only a dream could. Which is exactly what Jenna does when she takes a pictures. She lies. But tells lies that need to be told. She sits at the computer for hours adjusting exposure and tint and levels and contrast. Because she can say better than the truth. She can tell the picture more about itself than it can say. Which is what you want to do to the girl sitting alone and in shock outside the office. You want to adjust the image.

You see her there and try to imagine a picture. That she's not what she is. Because a picture can be unclear. She could just be a girl. Sitting. Waiting. Maybe just someone's sister. Someone's sister who's waiting to see a brand-new, baby niece. The goo-goo she'll make over the fresh smell of a tiny, shivering thing so new everyone is afraid to touch it. To hold it. Which is how the girl truly is. Something so changed everyone is afraid to touch. To come near. Quarantined. Like that bubble boy you heard about. Veiled in plastic and machines. Pressing his hands against his clear shell as if he were just a kid playing with wrappings and plastics ripped from presents on Christmas. Just a kid. Stuck inside. But if the plastic rips the air outside his shell would suck the oxygen out of him. A balloon that had been crushed against the ceiling at Jenna's son's birthday party, spitting out air. That one that started slinking back to the earth. Because things all lose air. Give in to gravity. Except pictures. Lies. To put her inside a lie. The boy's bubble. A clean, sterile hospital room where nothing is touched. Hurt. Inside a picture where nothing moves. Or to decide. To let her go. How one of the cowboys at the birthday party was leaving Jenna's house and his party balloon slipped from his fingers. Went into the air and further and further till it was a dot in the sky. A green dot. A mistake in the picture. And the unrelenting gunslinger started wailing. Wailing. Till his mother got so embarrassed she picked him up and started spanking him. With his too-big hat falling on the lawn without the mom picking it up. Spanking harder than what seemed right with some of the other parents sort of shocked. With their usual red-flag awareness. Spanking while carrying him off to the car and the whole time the boy is pointing at the dot in the sky. Growing smaller. What Jenna said will happen to the sun. It's dwarfing. Dwarfing till the world is one still picture of cold. Of lying. Of white. How the history of every picture is the same. The pictures begin with meaning before becoming decorations. But as the people caught in them disappear the meaning does too. Lies. The dreams you wake from in the middle of the night. With your intentions to tell them. To someone. Anyone.

And this is the dream you want to tell her. Sitting in the hall. Frozen. With the sounds of the hospital worriless and unending about her. As you try to put the girl into focus the way a man at a carnival says he can guess your weight. Like how you put your face to glass at the aquarium you went to with Jenna and her son, trying to decipher grammar of what will always live beneath the surface. Never finding air. Of what has learned to live without it. What fills itself with an evergreen liquid. With its thread of scales, the fish Jenna's son got painted on his face in the gift shop. How he kept making kissing and sucking faces like a fish. With his eyes bugging. Pretending to float. A dream. How there's a dream you're trying to tell her. Sitting beside her in the hallway. Without moving. You could be an old couple waiting together for a table at a restaurant. As you pull the paper hearts you took off the hospital wall from your pocket. How you try stuffing them in her hand. Try putting them in her hand only to watch them slip from her, grip-less. At your feet. All around your feet like the shred of broken balloons, rose petals, as if you'd surprised her for no reason. For a forgotten anniversary. How the paper seemed to unravel on the floor. Making a kind of crinkling sound in the air. That fake cricket sound inside a card a nurse was showing her friend. And you want to tell her you'd never give her something like that. Looking down at all the red paper on the hospital floor. Thinking of how the paper seemed to be opening. Blooming. Slowly.

REFRIDGERATOR

They say a Chinese boy was stuffed into a small refrigerator in the kitchen of Shen Li's Fortune Moon Restaurant because he saw something the owners didn't want him to see. They stuffed him in it and played cards. They played with the sharp, quick elliptic of their shouting and smoke and the clucking of caged chickens and with the cook chopping vegetables among steaming pots and frying pans and chairs scuffing the kitchen floor and American money tossed all over and a colored, joker card pinned against the forehead of one mobster laughing some oddly high-pitched laughing and banging inside the refrigerator, banging and banging, and a woman cook coming in to help prepare drinks for the mobsters saying "what's that banging" to the other cook in Chinese and him saying "they put the boy in the refrigerator" to her and she feels her stomach drop out. She feels her stomach drop out because she knows the boy is blind so he couldn't have seen anything at all but if she says anything at all they might stuff her in the refrigerator too. BANG, BANG. And she's pouring drinks into lime-colored cups with cherry blossom trees hand-painted on them and she looks at the clock on the wall yellowed with years of cigarette smoke and cooking and god knows what else. She looks at the walls thinking about the boy in the refrigerator and how the bumps of paint on the walls look like faces. Like faces trapped permanently in the purgatory of white walls and how one afternoon she washed dishes alone and thought that the bumps of paint were really the faces of her ancestors watching her and encouraging her and telling her not to give up and throw herself off the bridge she walks over every night on her way home from work carrying brown bags of food to stuff her face with in her one-room apartment where she has nothing on the walls but a David Bowie poster even though she's never even heard a song by David Bowie in her life. Even though her husband, still in China, would beat her for having a David Bowie poster which is probably the only reason she has a David Bowie poster at all. Why live in America if you're not doing something your husband would beat you for?

And that's how it always goes for her in America. Like just before she got to work. She's sitting down unwrapping a sandwich she got from a vending machine at a shop by the bus stop. The bus that takes her to the other side of town where she still has to walk ten or twelve blocks to get to Fortune Moon. A chicken sandwich. She's sitting down to eat it and while she's eating it she sees some kind of red tendon thing sticking out of the meat and she's trying her best to pick it out. She's trying her best but it's hard to pick it out and now her fingers have been digging too deep into the chicken and it makes her sick enough to throw it away. So she throws it away and also throws away the clear wrapping and the little, plastic tray the sandwich was in. And now she's thinking of the people whose whole job it is to make little, plastic trays. And then she's thinking of the people whose job it is to make the wrapping to cover the trays in. And then the people who inscribe the tiny, nutritional facts on the wrapping. And then the people who make the ink that the other people who write the nutritional facts on use. And that's how it goes for her. She's always hungry and sick at the same time here. She sees the thread of tiny things becoming bigger things. Big like the big women she has to ride the bus with every day. The ones who don't think she speaks English. Who call her Lucy Liu.

Big. All the big, cursive lettering on their glittery shirts. Complaining about the Spanish guy hosing off the sidewalk. "Motherfucker," they say. "These are new Jordans." "Jordan." "He played basketball." "You know what basketball is?" "You speak English? "El Jordon-o play-o basketball-o, motherfucker." And they stay that way the whole ride. Complaining. Their bellies hanging out of the tops of their too-tight jeans. The varying colors of their same-style sneakers. The black alphabets of names tattooed on their necks. Complaining. About men lost. About children crying. And then they get this look in their eye. They'll be giggling and laughing and arguing with the bus driver and dancing in the aisle singing some new song on the radio like they do every day and then they'll remember that she's sitting on the back of the bus. "Lucy," they yell at her in the back of the bus. "Lucy, you better be bringing us some sweet and sour chicken tomorrow." And she looks up at them and smiles. "Yes," she says back at them and that gets them laughing. "Yes, yes, yes," they say. Squinting their eyes. Hysterical. "Yes, yes, yes."

And she sits there staring out the bus window at the coke factory sputtering into a dark cloud of ashy smoke that's been hanging in the horizon for days now. They'd been talking about it on TV. How they didn't know what contaminants were in the cloud and the mayor and other people were threatening to close it down. America. She thinks of what her father would say about her living here when she pulls out the photographs she'd taken of herself at a photo booth in the mall. How each of the four pictures were the same. Exactly the same. And not once did she smile. Even with the electronic voice inside the machine telling her to get ready for the picture. She just sat there staring at the dot on the other side of the booth. Just sat there looking at the dot long after the booth was done taking pictures of her. And it seems to her now that she's always like that. Exactly how the dead look in old photographs. How their expressions seem to know everything and nothing at all.

And when she gets off the bus her face hatchets the wind. She walks and walks feeling as if the trees are burning behind her. Incinerating. She walks and is tangled by the invisible ropes and masts of air. She feels floating. Feels jolted. Like a Chinese, Wonder Woman in her translucent jet. Fondling the see-through gears and buttons of her air ship. Like routes only the blind boy from work knows. The shortcuts he traces by memory. By hand. And she's walking. Past houses where TV is the only window. Past an empty factory whose thousand some windows hold the whole orange weight of the setting sun. This long-hand of light. How it seems to write the world slower at the end of day. Branches charred against the empty sky. With the algorithm of the sidewalks. With the cracks in their pattern. The sudden and quickly recovered trip over uneven concrete. Hiccups of graffiti. Old wrappers cutting themselves out of the earth like wildflowers below the broken eggshells of clouds. Clouds like old newspaper bunched into balls for a fire. Clouds and air. That walkie-talkie buzz of air obsessed with its own voice. The kneeling of stoops and lights. How glass seems to vanish with the clarity of nightfall. And the world turns oil-colored and in-between. Turns illegitimate and cardboard tasting. Turns like the red valentines of leaves in the broken wineglass wind. Turns marginalized. And she's walking. Past an old fountain that's covered in clear plastic. Past the trailer park that's below the red-blue roller-coaster all the kids in town ride all summer long. Past chain restaurants with the space capsule of her heart floating far past the strain of gravity and into the frostbite colors of beyond. Past beyond. Because she's always sick and hungry here. Always walking. Always walking with the percolating rhythm of the red-blue-plumed city. The flags hanging from doorways like pelts. Like old curses. Like lecturing parents who never let their pointed fingers fall down. Like a lone glacier floating further and further and further out into water and melting and melting and melting. Like her. Walking. How she's suddenly wet. Melting. Wet thinking of the black man she saw playing classical music for a dozen or so elderly people outside the library one afternoon. His broad shoulders. His hands. A song she couldn't recognize. How it made her imagine him grabbing her by the shoulders. Pushing her against the wall. With all those people on the computers inside the library. Asking questions. The way people used to trust each other. Trusting now in their favorite companion. Their electric talisman. How she still remembers the first computer she ever saw. How she had to wait for images. They'd start at the bottom or in the middle. They'd start and you'd have to wait. An image came feet-first. Waiting and modem sounds. And she's waiting for an image now. An answer. She's waiting and wishing she had a cell phone. Wishing she had a cell phone so she could pretend to talk on it. Pretend to talk on it the way the white girls do when they're alone. When they're avoiding someone. Because no one, no one, no one can see her desire. Because she's walking. She's climate-controlled. Automatic. With the crass sting of sweat in her eyes. With her memories like old, blue tins an old woman keeps her knickknacks in. Knickknacks made in China. Tins made in China. Everything made in China. America made in China. America, land of Chinese knickknacks. Land of the many hours she spent alone in her room crossing and uncrossing her legs. Crossing and uncrossing. And now she's walking into Shen Li's Fortune Moon. She's putting her coat on the rack and getting ready for them. Their hands. How they bark "whore" at her in Chinese. And she's walking to the kitchen and says "what's that banging" to the other cook. He tells her it's the boy. The boy is locked in the fridge. And a word forms. A word forms inside her like a bright, pink scar while she pours their drinks. And she's turning to them now. And she's ready. She's stopped walking. Stopped moving.

She stops.

CITY

There are crude repairs happening in parallel infrastructures. Huge, white, industrial curtains covering the dilapidated, street level entrances. Curtain-white over the hurt-white of buildings. Broken, skyscraper windows open in the unhinged wind. With the missing steps inside the belly of the infrastructures like bones inside of whales. Going up through offices that haven't been used in years. Wires hanging from the enamel-colored ceilings. Like jungle vines. Like the shadows of jungle vines. Like the sketches long vines make when artists tie pencils to the ends of them. Scratching. Scratching. Scratching. And the ham radio, ghost voices inside. Desks and chairs stacked inside of closets. Like men trapped inside the bellies of whales. Their feet submerged in black water. Sitting at tables lit by candles made from whale fat. The sea sounds they live with. The sea.

And I want to yell a pearly thing. A hundred chandeliers falling thing through all the grate steam below. Because a correction seems mandatory. I see numbers bubbling themselves everywhere. Numbers in beams and the conclusions of blocks and signs. Lines threading into lines that crisscross over the streets in trapeze. That vein and carry. That error. And I'm pleading for a frontal life. An exposure. But the city is a spy. It's always behind me.

It's calculating the sum and subtraction of numbers. It's parting numbers. And the numbers aren't parting in my favor. They're upside-down in a mismatched, barcode transformation. They're making their color known in the sky.

So I spend hours disputing the ladders. The fire escapes branching in fluke. In lame tedium. Because when a fire happens here the sky takes blackened everything in. Soured, melted couches and all. Takes that square of living and adjusts it. Tweaks it. Rearranges it. Because there is an order to living in the air. Whole, charred places sucked into the almost-sky. Into invisible life. The city's lost apartments and demolished buildings and bulldozed tombstones in a kind of tightrope walk above us. In finished, un-heckled grace. In a sort of soft Z sound I can always hear without much effort.

"Z," the sky says. Z with a kind of salesman lingering. With all the horrid otherwise of bus stops and coatrooms and unsmiling days and nights and red velvet walls. Z and I'm taking this opportunity to tell you that I'm real. I'm real now and I'm still looking for you. You and the belly of the whale you're inside. Z with the anxiety of white cars. White as the mouth of a whale turned over by the fisherman's strange and violent contraptions into the black-heart water. White as the pupils of the life-sized, cardboard cutouts of you someone has made and put around town. In alleys. In windows. Alone and strange and everywhere. How there must a whole factory of them. How a man was carrying a cardboard version of you in the subway. I yelled for him but he disappeared behind white columns. Yelled as the train came screaming in with its comb of windows. With Z. With the memory of you like a white owl wrapped inside my coat. With you making these miserable owl sounds. Hooting with everyone looking at me with cracked, lime green plastic faces. With their dialed faces. With everyone looking at me on the subway with their rotary phone faces ringing that terrible, horrible ring that phones used to make when we were kids and even before we were kids. And I'm jumping out the door at the next stop. And I'm jumping over turnstiles and up onto the street to birdbath with the air and the light.

And I'm thinking of you. You like all the places that have been empty too long. That melancholy of vacant rooms in famous hotels. All the unused chairs in airplanes and movie theaters and subway cars. What could they possibly tell us about ourselves that we don't already know? How I'm looking at the street for some kind of insight. I'm watching the rain fall lackadaisically from a crumbling fire escape. With outside stretched before me as far as I can see from where I am now. Which isn't far. And I'm thinking of you. Thinking of everyone I've ever lost because I want to tell them something that I've learned. How somehow I'd gotten to where I am now either because of them or in spite of them. And there are things they've taken that I want back. And I'm willing to beg, to plea, and to reconcile. Because there's still some sort of inarticulate lesson to be explained.

Or is there? Maybe there's nothing left to say. Maybe there's no search party out for me after all. Maybe it's just them and just me. All in our own place. Like automatic lamps turning on and off in the winter homes of old couples off to Florida for the year.

How all this gets me thinking of what life would look like without me in it. Some dock below the Brooklyn Bridge where the engine of an unmanned taxicab is running and running and running. Some hill where children should have been playing. Where the silhouette of a boy I do not know is patterned against the sky, wondering if he can take the steep ride down. Some street at the end of August where two people might have been kissing. Where doors swung open and drunks slid past without a word. Chased off into the night like birds from screaming children. Some hospital bed where only the droning of machines catch a kind of almost cry. Where hand prints streak themselves across the window of a maternity nursery like cheesy special effects in a remake of The Invisible Man.

How it all makes me want to tie bandages about my body like the Invisible Man. Because I want to be seen where I am. For what I am. I want to wrap bandages around my body until someone studies me long enough to do the unraveling for me. Understands me enough to turn away tie after tie. Till I'm invisible again. Because wasn't that an old dream of ours. To not be seen. To spy on the people we hate and love. To know exactly what they do when no one is looking. To understand why everyone seemed so different. How difference seemed like the only thing that could possibly be true.

Difference like sci-fi. Like the red and gunmetal colored UFOs someone has been spray-painting all over the city. That huge one painted in a vacant lot behind the bank. "Take me with you," written above it. How it all makes me remember you. How you once pointed at the moon and told me it was four minutes away. Always four minutes. How you told me that if aliens were watching us from a thousand light years away they wouldn't be watching us. They'd be seeing Earth a thousand years ago. And I couldn't believe it. Because it meant that no matter how far away you can go there'll be an echo of us, an afterimage. That everything we do is reflected by distance. And distance follows distance.

Like that cat I saw pawing at another cat inside a corner store window. Scratching and pawing against the glass. Trying not to get its tail wet in the rain. Trying not to get hit by the small stones some boys hanging out at the newsstand were throwing at it. How at first I thought it was pawing at its own reflection. Which seemed somehow sadder. But I think now it was sadder that there were two. Two both knowing what they were missing. Which reminds me of you. How looking out at the sometimes dark-red and mostly-green water below the bridge at night I feel I can hear a whale song below it. That sonogram-like murmuring below the surface. How when I find a cold, high place I think I can see the outline of the monster stewing below. Like Jaws. Like some black leviathan whose mouth opens to what you think of when you're afraid of God. That opens to you.

And did I mention how I opened? How they hit me in

the subway. Hit me and I stripped my pants down to my knees. How I was looking for you. I swear I was looking for you but it felt so good to be naked there. With their hand between their legs. On my bare ass. With people watching. Because I was open. Open like a kind of hurt and the smell of something burning that never goes away. That feeling of your thick lips in the dark so long ago. That smell of you all over. And I swear I was looking. When they hit me. With the white and smash of winter skies in colorless photos. Those pictures of people in your family who were alive before anyone you've ever known was born. Hit me and I heard the whales singing through each and every street. Heard the subway cars screeching to a halt. Heard windows busting and you coming. I heard you coming in a sad way. Like the color red on anything when it rains. How they dragged me from the subway and took me to the jail. That place of orange following orange. Of our zoo sounds holding over blue floors. Blue walls. Holding and someone is pounding a brick against an iron slot for help. For one of the skinhead guards. You hear him and then screaming. With us living our life of makeshift things. Of hiding. Of permanently marking the skin with something to remind us there's something outside and below the skin. Something beyond the blue walls. Blue but there was red there too. There was more than a fair share of red. And maybe that's just it. Maybe life isn't a story about us. About someone. Maybe life is just a series of colors. Colors and whatever comes with them. Like the old things that they give back to us when we leave the jail. So long separated that they're not even ours anymore. Just things. Just colors.

Like how one afternoon it all just sort of made sense. With that female guard. That one who really liked me. How she took me to an old part of jail that hadn't been used in years. Took me even though she could have gotten fired for it. Took me just so I could stand in front of an open window and look down at the water. Because it seemed like that was the most human thing she was capable of doing. And that's it. You understand what I'm saying?

That's it.

MY MORNING SONG IS BETTER THAN YOURS

THE ROOM

Light is the oldest thing, says the room. *This is your window.*
Outside: the voices of the dead have come back burning.
What we call light. How it dreads the worn shoulders of
the sky, our open mouths, what sings as sun.

~

You want an image. You want a bare wall to hang a
painting of a woman sitting in the gold ocean of a field.
You want to place your daughter in front of that paint-
ing, asking: *Is that you, mommy? Is that you?*

~

The constant sound of someone's hand turning the knob.
This throttling of keys.

~

You're staring back at me with my eyes again. Your palms
opening inside my chest.

~

The universe is suddenly left-handed. You're painting

cube upon cube. What was abstraction in its largeness is now profoundly singular. A single. Yet the single has a smaller counterpart. It is like those borders of the alphabet hanging from the walls of a classroom. *A a, B b, C c, D d.* For every capital there is a non-capital. *YOU* is always followed by you who is experiencing exactly what *YOU* is experiencing in smaller doses. *YOU* is a room. There is a smaller room of you that *YOU* can barely fit inside.

~

There is this naming based upon selection. You call this *bedroom* because you've placed a bed inside it. *Bathroom* because of the actions that take place there. Why does the furniture hold such precedence?

~

This is the room of *not touching*. It is always happening, not happening.

~

How one dwells in the room never knowing they're being answered.

~

It is spring in the room. There are bags packed on the floor. I am staring out at the trees as I often have when I had nothing to say. She is leaving. I look at the trees, the roof-lines, the sky. She is leaving and I have nothing to say.

~

This is the room where air kisses the spark. The spark turns into and around itself before bursting into a flame. The flame seeks, tangling upward, becoming a fire. The fire howls in the air becoming a blaze. The air tosses the blaze about until it spreads wildly into many blazes becoming an inferno. The inferno defines nothings. It is the opposite of definition. It is the pattern of what once was the room. It un-shapes. Everything that was the room vanishes into thin air. Air remains constant. You breathe it into your lungs. Your lungs which are rooms of air.

~

There is some unseen pattern that allows your heart to beat. Air again. It is streaming through everything. You wonder what the world would look like if air had a color. Strange hues streaming from people's mouths. You wonder if people would exhale different shades when they lied. You wonder if the air would change around two people falling in love. Perhaps this would change everything. Perhaps we wouldn't exist.

~

I am no longer now that he is. She holds her stomach like a green bird, buried lightning.

~

Tiny cry. You fill the room. You suck on my skin looking for milk. You bruise.

~

We hold you below the light like an open chest. *Whose nose? Whose eyes?*

~

This is painting of a woman holding a newborn child. Whose face is that erasing like gold below the falling snow? *I'm leaving*, she said. *You would not like what this city has done to me. My memories must be someone else's. A dream. Do you feel it?*

~

Acorns falling against the cobblestone. That's how I remember you.

~

Nurses spread her legs. She opened. You came as a bell. You came and we kissed you and we recorded us kissing you. We watched the recording of us kissing you. Our kisses came back to us like the sound of shredding paper.

~

This is the gracelessness we belong to. This and the yellow stairwell always filled with smoke. Here in the room. Here in hinges. Here in brushing shoulders without speaking. Folding laundry on the floor. You look up at me, and say: "_____ ." And I say: "_____ ." And it goes on like this. Settled.

~

Diverging of birds, in *wasn't*, in *mistook*. We could be. *Could be*: as if holding *once* like the eye of bird. All rooms opening into another until there is no room.

~

Square is ?. Four lines. A shape. We write out our grocery list on a ? of paper.

--green cabbage	*--garlic*
--potatoes	*--carrots*
--onions	*--2 heads of broccoli*

Lists and etc. You put a ^ on top of ■ and get the etc. of house. Etc. of roof leaks, tip-tap of rain in pots, a broken hammer. Etc. of old paint cans, ash trays filling and emptying, dead leaves in the doorway. Etc. of the baby cries, of TV channels, of e-mails. Etc. of the toilet flushes, light switches, the alarm clock. Etc. of *I love you*. Etc. of *I will*.

I Will as if the ■ of a mirror. Dormant but revolving on the foundation of *I*. You keep changing sides. You say: *the windows are dusty. Someone's been running their fingers through the dust.*

~

You lie the same way you eat. I've watched you. You stick a piece of meat on your fork and spin it in front of you, looking it over, never swallowing.

~

No snow falls beneath the bridge. You are the bridge.

~

Daughter: stands on a chair pretending to be a statue. I move her arms. Motionless where I put them. I make them wave. I make them pray. I use two fingers to make her lips smile, pout, tremble.

Mother: doesn't watch, her back turned in the painting.

~

Offering *the* as itself, in its own movement. How *the* illustrates like the opening of curtains. A *the* for us. This *us* in *us*.

~

Small colors becoming small landscapes in small things. *Everything I told you that would happen has come true.*

~

You turn to me. Gold light falls to the floor like a broken cage.

~

You turn to me. Every side of the room is a mirror. We see ourselves repeating.

~

You turn to me. I can barely fit inside us.

~

You turn to me.

THICK RIB OF

THE LAMENTATION ANIMAL

To rub one part of *I* against another to create music.

This violin of oneself, this rough strum of *I*, arc of wing over thick rib. This masturbatory chirping like the meat of God clenched in your teeth, an apostrophe giving aloneness possession over the inarticulate, a bridge be-tween chords.

Fugues of *I* divide into layers of sound.

Grass hums.

~

Antenna of *I* bob like a TV with legs smashing its ma-chine head against a wall. TV is not lamentation. TVs are formulated by a principle of equal opportunity. *I* resemble them only in blankness. Their music siphons static for mimicry and brings filth back to the fly. I forms its own harping.

~

I is the key of the thick rib.

Incessant collisions with *I*, always of *I*, *I* the eternal stranger. Do not deny it. Transcendence is the fallacy of music. Sing love. Love is a burglar in the house of *I*. Marriage is an exchange of voices in repetition, in echoes, in tonal dependence. Widowing is the gospel of *I* mourning itself. Death of *I* gives a quiet voice back to the multitudes. Lamentation burrows in the mouth of its widow.

There is nothing beyond what the thick rib says.

I is never.

I is born below its own avalanche.

MY MORNING SONG IS

BETTER THAN YOURS

We made a game out of telling each other stories and the only way to win the game was to end it by saying: … *then you realized you were on another planet.* I like games like that. I just wish I could have been clearer about the shape of us reflected in the black of the TV that wasn't on. I just wanted you to know how slow everything moved in there. Like tar all over you. Like what you only kind of hear when you sleep outside.

~

Bitch, they say, is a good word for the dog-red gums of the sky. I say *bitch* when there is some static in the air. We go whirling in it. And I just feel so bad like sinking my teeth into something really soft but hard enough to take it.

~

I hear it most in the getting-up. My life talking on the other end of sleep. How it boils over into a slow mess in the window's sun. How the sun coming in here is coming in different than it would anywhere else in the world. It is bubbling up in front of me. Rising like I don't know what. And the worst of it being the *I don't know what* of it. Because I just really don't know.

~

So you're driving and driving and driving. And it's a long road. And there's no one on it. And it's the middle of the night. And you're driving and driving and driving. And then, all of a sudden...

~

And I just want to say that my morning song is better than yours. I want you to hear it buzzing in me like an old radiator. I want you to do what you've done before. To press your ear against the skin and listen for the static.

~

I go. Gone being accounted for. Because even as I sit here I am gone. But going is here. I see it across the room like a shadow I haven't made yet. One that stretches like yet. *Yet* like a mouth inside a mouth that runs its teeth against its teeth. I grind my teeth on their other set. Which means there must be a word behind my every word. Because a mouth with two sets of teeth must have two tongues.

~

What I mean is that the closer you get the harder it is to see. And it's so hard to see when you draw me near.

~

I had a toy. He was an action figure with a red beard. I liked him so much that my mom bought me two of him. So how can I account for the fact that one of them is missing both his legs and the other is fine? Why is it I lost the one with legs but the one without is still in my dresser drawer?

~

All quantification is justification. Just wait and see when it adds up.

~

There was a picture of you and that picture hurt me more than anything can say. Even though the picture didn't do anything. It didn't move. It was just standing all in lipstick in an apartment but it hurt me. It hurt me because it was young. It hurt me because it had never even thought to think of me.

CRIMINALS

What about the goons?

Those criminals thwarted and left for dead in every ac-
tion movie for the past thirty years. I'm sure at least a
dozen survived the slaughters. This one who quit work-
ing for Colombian drug smugglers is now an insurance
salesman who makes his kids say the Pledge of Allegiance
every morning. Or this one, with a trachea, in some VA
Memorial Hospital in New Jersey. He sits by the window
in his wheelchair holding the wooden figurines of ani-
mals he made in a whittling class. He hates the shade of
green of his hospital gown. It reminds him of how water
always looks in the rivers and lakes up north. He knows
how good water can hide what we want lost. He knows
water is the greatest liar. He'll tell you never trust a man
who takes a shower more than twice a day. He'll tell you
failure is like cancer. He'll tell you that it always comes
long before anyone notices and once they do it's too late.

~

Light is the builder.

Your entire world is shaped by light. It frees and confines.
You say the crime happened in *broad daylight*. Why is this

surprising? What does the light in its narrowness or its thickest have to do with safety? What reflects, what illuminates, does not restrain us. It is not a basis of conduct.

You have nothing to say about coarse shadows.

~

There is no difference between saving the world and destroying it.

This is why the policeman seems to lovingly embrace the felon he's pinned to the concrete. This is why the hero rarely murders his arch nemesis. Each movement of good vs. evil makes little difference. We battle routine. We battle the slow burn of time. We fight with what little wisdom we've gathered from experience.

We tell ourselves we're good.

FALL APART STUFF

I will pick up the mess soon. The fall apart stuff. Dry, thin spaghetti noodles sprawled across the floor.

I will hike up the plain dress and get a piece of glass stuck in my kneecap I won't get out for days.

He had drunk sloppy and passed out in our bed.

He is snoring inside the silo of his throat. The inside there shines golden but that's not the truth. There is something caught below the gold.

~

I'm hiding under a bed. It's an old style bed. There are springs coming out below the mattress. If you hold on to them you'll be safe. They might thrash the bed about but holding on you'll slide across the wooden floor. It works because you are small enough. They will toss it around violently until they give up, coughing the hallway bloody.

They will die soon after.

~

He is a room without walls floating across a flat lake in the dark. The only light there comes from a lamp on the table inside the room. It brings silver, black-eyed sharks up from the green, black bottom to circle. You see the sharp fins cutting around the room like saws coming through the floor in cartoons. But the room doesn't fall through like Daffy Duck. It goes on and they follow?the room sliding away from us in sections. A pattern synchronized like still pictures in a kid's flip book.

~

The bathroom mirror is a Picasso face in harsh red paint. You'll need stitches on the hook of your nose and on the eyelid. It hangs there limp like a white, wet petal cut loose with gray scissors.

I look for my dimples before I realize I never had any.

Smiling, I think those were my sister's.

~

Bowlegged, you sit on the toilet and look out the window. It's morning, hours before he will wake into the stillness. The dreamy, menstrual sky lashes violent lava from its black mouth. On the clothes line, you'll see two fresh curtains catch the wind like a pair of big lungs.

The black-n-blue trees stay still and sore in the quivering grass.

YOLK

This is the soft middle of it, yolk-colored, as undeniable as frowning, against music, as this it becomes a girl, as this girl becomes a body, raped and murdered, becomes light, becomes a note plucked from the staves of railroad. How later, as a salesman is painting her name on every windshield on every car in the lot, in memorial, painting her name the exact color of candlelight, a mechanic is writing the instructions on how to start a car right on its passenger door so the mechanic on the next shift will have an idea of how to start it. Because something is wrong with its engine, with its insides, like my mother's appendix, like my brother's bank account, like the slate-colored eyes of a homeless, skateboarder who's talking about the Mayan calendar at the six-pack shop, with his stack of secondhand books under his arm, with his fresh tattoo bandage unraveling, because something is wrong. Wrong, like how that woman who stole a knife at the pizza shop last Saturday stabbed at her stomach and arms in the bathroom, screaming I have AIDS at the cops, like a psychopathic version of the owl from those old lollipop commercials: how many licks does it take? How we're trying to open ourselves from the outside. How we're counting each stroke and each crack. Because there has to be a center, has to be a way inside, has to be being the last form of prayer, the viscera of desire. How

desire is: the stung cup we drink from; the ology of our-
selves imagined; the language of strays hiding inside the
pile of trash in the work trailer beside our house, yowl-
ing all night; the pictures in frames turned upside-down
throughout; and all the people you cut from them; and
you, mostly naked, searching for the title to your car; how
you said it was going to rain; told me there was a trick
to knowing it; the rain; because you can always see the
white side of the leaves; just before; the rain; you can see
always see their bellies; their middles; their soft insides.

MR. WATSON, DO YOU REMEMBER HOUSES?

The Scientists on the street points out things to the brain machine. The brain floats in its chamber, wires threaded through it, perched atop a machine of robotic legs. It clanks and clanks and the scientists watch it swish around in green liquid trying to understand whether it is coming on its own accord or simply following the scientists out of instinct.

"Mr. Watson, do you remember these? These are called houses."

The brain machine hesitates and its thoughts transfer to the scientist's handheld computers: "A swim across... she was there...peal...there was a cramp in my leg. My mother in a blue apron, meaning the taste of apricot, tires sliding over rain, the rain sliding beneath us...water... a house, yes, a house by the sea... ember, a perfect white sweater...people were dancing on the hardwood floors..."

The scientists ask again: "Mr. Watson, do you remember houses?"

The brain machine walks closer to a blue house on the corner. White petals cover the sidewalk. It stops, petals floating and bouncing off its glass encasing. Inside the house, an old woman sits alone at a table staring down at a white mask. She sticks an empty spoon into the mask's mouth and the toothless opening bites down.

She does this until the mask seems full. She then picks up the mask and walks to a door and opens it.

It is a closest filled with white masks.

She throws the mask to the others and they devour it the way lions devour a gazelle.

She shuts the closet door.

THE HOUSE IS A PLACE WHERE THINGS CAN GO WRONG

The first family came upon the first house and took life there. They dragged their life in like the leaves drag all other leaves behind them. Still, the life was heavier than it sounds, heavier than paper scraping. The life was a body of wet leaves they dragged in that got up and moved. There were wet footprints through the house all the time like someone just got out of the shower. The smell of the body was pleasant, autumnal. Still, in certain lights, the body was menacing when it stood motionless for a long time at the top of the stairs. Sometimes it would blow apart in the white kitchen as if it were angry. It gave the first family the feeling they lived among white trees that blocked all other things. The first children would wake sometimes pulling leaves out of their little throats.

The second family has a child who projects images from a small hole her head.

If children play near the second house the girl will go to the front window and project herself near the children which scares the real children away. The girl then walks through the house hitting her stomach violently. She projects an image of herself crying and stares at it crying. They sob into each other, the girl's hand trying to hold the light.

At night, the second mother stands above her bed and the hole in the girl opens like an eye, pouring light onto the ceiling. A figure in a white dress and crown waves in front of a castle, melting maybe, and the figure is laughing and crying and screaming all at once.

The third family was comprised of strangers. The father was old and thin with young, chubby children. His wife was an attractive but worn woman in her thirties. They would wake every morning and sit at a table in a room that turned different shades of green depending on the time of day. They would ask each other: *who are you, where did we come from, why do you attach yourself to me?* The old man and his wife would rake their lawn and their presence would make the neighbors uncomfortable. Men in suits would drive past the old man on their way to work and he would give them a helpless look, like a dog asking for food or a child who had been separated from his mother and left in a shop. The old man's children were like greedy birds. You'd see them walking to school sometimes in the very early mornings eating something they found on the side of the road. They looked at you like things without eyes yet when you left them you still felt as though you were being watched.

The fourth house is a year of broken window, pills swallowed. It is an alley that forms in the house where a deaf man sings what he imagines is a song. The fourth house is a bag lady's hands pouring onto the ground and then growing into the center of the fifth house: two giant, white hands erupting from the living room floor that spasm like trapped birds. The fifth father takes an ax to them and begins hacking them apart. He cannot explain why he feels that what he's doing is wrong and why he hears screaming from someplace far away. Meanwhile, in the fourth house, the deaf man takes a needle out of the bag lady's leg. She's brushing her hair with the cuffs of her coat. She's slumped against the wall, looking at her feet like she's won a prize.

In the sixth house there's a large wall which separates an old man from his teenage self. There's a tiny slot in the wall between them which allows the two to exchange notes the size of human fingers. These exchanges always involve the boy asking questions which the old man carefully erases and sends back through the wall. The boy reads each blank scrap as through he's gotten dumped by a girl at the high school dance. The boy puts on a sad record and lies in his bed looking at the ceiling. The old man sits listening to the muffled sounds of the record though the wall, tapping his foot, mumbling something he remembers. What the old man sings is never a part of the song. The young man doesn't sing.

The seventh house is aware of itself and therefore hates itself. It feels the little boy inside it move things, run, spill spice on to the floor. Everything is replaced in it: windows, candles, appliances, floors. The boy becomes a man inside the house and then becomes a ruined thing. He holds a knife against his throat in a mirror and cuts and cuts. The mirror becomes a kind of red sky, another house, walls the boy can live inside. The house loses the boy. The boy was a red dream the house had. The boy was a red bridge with two ends and the feeling you were waving your hands at every edge trying your best not to fall. The house coughs the boy's blood and swallows it through each mirror. It hates itself more and more, drop by drop by drop.

The eighth house is being graded on qualities of abreaction and memory and its inability to distinguish each. For example, if house says "the clouds outside are crumbs in a cardinals mouth" it would be judged poorly whereas if it said "I remember the old woman who lived here, her skin which smelled like boiled water" it would receive no grade as the old woman was nothing but tissue paper kids once tore apart. It would also be deducted points for dirt it seems to hide like food and the birds in the attic without beaks. The birds smile at each other in the dark, showing human teeth.

The ninth house repeats its own name like a pop song. It is a pop song, old pictures from the seventies the kid's father never looks at, a sad kid in his room looking at the wall. The lyrics of the house are the fingernail marks around the parent's bed, swirls of them, like gull tracks. The lyrics are the dull eyes of the sister in her wheelchair who does not talk, does not move, yet sometimes touches her privates in front of people when they visit the house, opening her skirt to them, forming a face her mother cannot understand, her mouth opening like a needle touching a groove.

The tenth house attaches itself to the neighbor's house, sucks on it, deflates it. The inside of the tenth house grumbles, unsatisfied. In its center, the belongings of the other houses coalesce, covered in a thick film of stomach acid which slowly melts them away. The family does not live in the tenth house. They are bones which move as the tenth house moves. They are the constant creaking of doors which in itself is a kind of hunger no man or house can understand. Doors open. You hinge. The dark tries to tighten the rivet in your throat but you still make the same horrible sounds.

The eleventh house is a lost toy. It is you telling yourself a dream at your kitchen table, the wire hangers clattering in the empty fridge, the thin transparent meat they hold. *In the dream,* you say, *a girl was hiding you underwater below a machine that was shredding fish. In the dream,* you say, *an old woman carried you and small animals on a floating book across a sea. In the dream, you say, a body was hanging from a rope in the town square but no one noticed. They were smiling and laughing but when the body finally fell they all ran away.* In the eleventh house, you can't sleep. You fold your arms against your chest like a corpse. You make a house of cards which is never a house of cards. It is always your body, sleeping. It is your body which has always been a small boat ready to drift away.

You are in the eleventh house. You are repeating yourself. Your father is standing at the window holding the pieces of every widow you ever broke. He is mumbling to the window, repeating himself. He is saying something about windows to the child playing in the yard. The child is you repeating your life and your father is watching, mumbling, repeating. He is trying to tell you not to make the same mistakes but he can't. He is helpless. He cradles the glass which is cool like sand at night but leaves his arms full of tiny little cuts. He sees the child running. He knows what happens next. The child will become a window. The window will shatter and there will be a new child, a new window. He will never see through them. There are no windows. There are blurs of light, obstructions, broken glass. He repeats himself as the glass cuts deeper into his arms: *there are no windows.*

The twelfth house is burning down even though there is no fire inside it. A black river of smoldering wood rushes through the walls. An old woman in a wooden chair melts into it, incinerates to the floor. A child without a mouth crawls through the hallway as a room crumbles into itself. This is the last song I heard you sing. The twelfth house is your bad singing. You're on the stage with your electric guitar. The crowd is embarrassed for you. I am looking at you as if I am trying to turn you off. I am turning you off. I am always trying to turn you off.

The thirteenth house is a factory where men smoke as they work and never wear gloves. There's rain coming in from the roof somewhere and the windows are so dirty everything looks green and murky and underwater. There are dogs wandering around the factory. Everything is meat to them: chairs, tables, buttons, people. They gnaw at everything and everything gnaws back.

In the meat there's videotape. The workers rip it out of the flesh and hold the strips up against the florescent.

The workers write down what they see in the tape and sew the tape back in the meat and slam the meat back on the belt. The meat makes animal sounds from what was cut in them. The whole factory fills with their sounds. Dogs howl.

The fourteenth house is the fog erasing the morning, Satie's Trois Gymnopédies, the tiny fetuses of light growing inside the apples. It is the heartbeats which bleach the walls. It is all of California at night drawn on a single piece of paper. It is someone tracing that piece of paper with their finger in the dark. It is someone you lost floating away somewhere so deep in themselves their body will never find them again. Listen: you can hear whales. You can hear the blue light from which your body was made.

The fifteenth house is rain on Mars. It is space streaming off red sand. It is time opening the letter that invented sadness, true sadness, an old song you played that the ghetto kids made fun, saying: *turn that corny shit off.* It is the block piano chords on a day that is gray blur. The weird color and vividness the people make in the concrete color. How when the weather turns people erupt like weather. How I go to bed because the potential for violence makes me tired. I look into your eyes and it makes me tired. There is no such thing as eyes.

The houses congregate together, push apart. The houses spar and flay. I drink blonde and feel the artic, feel the river of ice moving away with the spring. I look at the houses which are dressed like churchgoers. The houses say "God bless you" and their doors bleed. The houses say "good morning" and the doors in the sky all close. You hear their knobs being turned by whatever is on the other side. You wonder if you can call what doesn't open a door.

The new house is different from the old house in that the new house hides its hands. It is quarrelsome. It is the half-blind dog staring down the driveway at the sun. It is the fat of the sky hanging lower than normal. It is my neighbors who are rats wearing skin or pigs who let rats live inside their eyes. They smile at me and fangs show, grass floats, skin falls to the ground. At night, they drag mud into their houses to roll around in, snorting. At night, you don't sleep for the wind which wails through the tunnels they've dug below the ground.

The old house is a shirt you're wearing. It is the blue the lake should be. It is more than a reflection. On your hip, a small TV screen in your skin turns on. We lie naked on the bed with my face between your legs. You moan sometimes and your breasts shake. The fields outside grow larger, grow further from the rest of the earth. The screen on your hip plays a game show. There's a woman on it with a bad perm laughing and clapping. There's always a winner. The bed shakes and the fields shake. You make a sound and it is almost like a cheer. You open your mouth, coming, clenching a little TV screen between your teeth.

I don't want to look at houses so I look at cones of light people's faces project. The cones are bright and flickering, prismatic. The people try to strip them from their faces like bear cubs with their heads trapped inside road cones. Meaning: this house is driving in a station wagon through Canada with you family in 1991. Your father points out the window and says: *look over there son, I am the type of father who shows you things and points.* You look over to where he is pointing. It's a trap.

Harm is a word which carries actual feeling. Harm is like the house in that way. It gathers a ball of feeling together and packs it tighter and tighter till the compression leads to expansion. Just look at the little boy here, dark-circled on the floor, growing out of himself. He is his mother's sudden rage. He is father's unwavering sadness. He is a trapped bird in the house. The parents look up at the ceiling, holding brooms, trying to find the sound in them that thumps and thumps and thumps.

The house is a radio station that plays metal clouds which drag across the road because they're too heavy for the sky. Sparks follow. The shadows and colors and fields you once dreamed about all come true. Who were we to the house but thin throats and the future, something which drew you out to the center of the woods? You turn the station and find another house, a first kiss. No, the first kissing, the kissing all kissing comes from. The world delays and I kiss you. I forgot to tell you how cold the woods could become.

The houses rarely remember the locksmith. How strange, really, to think there is someone with the tools to get inside of them. How it is the same with us: always one who can get in, one who doesn't have to ask. But fuck it, who cares? We are alone today in the house and the stars above us are like a million silver guitars thrown out to sea. Yeah, sure, space is a locked door too but I can hear the music sawing behind it, the wind in the hollow spaces, the flames.

There is just enough gold color here to help you forget there was a house. You move in the shine of it. It is like being on acid when you are a little too young for acid. It is like being in Vietnam when you born in 1985. I am scraping all these bats off a wall and the bats have all this gold ooze dripping out of them. The ooze is blood and the blood is a house. The blood is a McDonald's happy meal. You buy one and give it to your son. You buy it and he is content simply to hear *happy meal*. He opens his happy meal in the backseat. He pours a little graveyard out of the bag onto his lap. Little tombs get stuck in-between the leather seats like fries.

The houses on this street are our chewed fingertips—no substance in them. So we thread water in each other's mouths. We fuck with our faces pressed to the wall. We're so white our teeth are sugar.

Every leaf is the same ruined house she is trapped inside. Every leaf has the same small window in its center she waves to me from. When one snaps I hear her scream all the way down for what seems like days. There is sometimes so many of them falling at once I cannot hear anything else but her. At night, I don't sleep because I can't. I look up into the leaves. All the windows in the little houses hanging from the branches are still on. They are stars under stars. They are nightlights through the thrush.

The house is a tulip which means I am kissing you some-
place really soft. It means: there's legs and no body, walk-
ing and walking. You hear the heels dragging against the
floorboards and know the lack of body is making some-
one scared and sad. I hold the handle of the night to kiss
you better. You make a sound like the skin that parts you,
the skin that holds my hands intact.

The house is a gravel road. There are people walking down the road telling each other a story. The story is a house they're passing that they themselves sit inside, feeling the dark coming, telling each other a story about strangers walking along the road.

It occurs to the people on the road that they cannot remember a time before this walking. It occurs to the people inside that they are also outside, they can see themselves now from the window, and they feel all the little hands trying to push through their skin.

The house is blood I am washing from my hands. It is the shape of people where people should be, the shape that is there. You are holding the house. It is filled with pages that talk about houses. Look to the left of these pages, to the right. Look at the edges where the page drops off. You are drowning in a life. Call it life. It keeps going where yours ends.

This house only lasts three minutes on the 20th of June. Neighbors come out onto their porches to wait for it in the space where it used to be. It is nighttime and people are drinking beer and lighting firecrackers and eating barbeque. This year the house doesn't appear when it is supposed to and people murmur about it and get nervous and then forget about it. People get drunk and tired and go home.

Across the street from where the house should have appeared a man drinks alone. His wife is not there. She hadn't come home with him and though he'd asked everyone if they'd seen her they couldn't tell him where she'd gone. He knew though where she was and who she was with and that she wasn't coming home.

There is a shimmering across the street like a UFO and then the sky turns a bright orange.

He doesn't even see it. That or it is him this time that has disappeared, a new space where something used to be. A new space where time was.

This house is cutting off your black hair. It is the sound of scissors cutting. It is a god cutting away images from the world. It is cleaning the hair from the floor and holding it. It is burning your hair and stuffing it back into your mouth. No, you're just waking, burning, with clumps of hair missing. You're lying next to a body of hair tied together with rope. The birds outside are scissors cutting the air. The air is the ear of a small boy. You look through it.

What I meant to say earlier is that in this house there are five people who hang from your life like curtains. Each person's name is a curtain. Each person's name is how you've wronged someone you loved. You look at them and see a window. You look at them but see what is just behind their frame. When the wind blows they open. What comes next you call *glass*.

This house is an arrival to the house. There's a man at the door in a trench coat. He has teeth that hum like the blank screens of dead TVs. He is trying to sell us prosthetic parts though we insist we don't need any. This leads to a heated argument in which the man gets so mad his lips foam. We close the door in fear but the man refuses to relent. He peers at us through the windows as we shuffle around the tiled floor on the stumps where our arms and legs should be. He stares at us on the ground, huddled together, trying to dial the phone with our teeth. In the distance, wolves scream. The gazelles are ripping them apart.

Out of this house a man runs a business specializing in glow-in-the-dark women's apparel. He got the idea when he met his girlfriend who is see through in the dark. She walks through the house and coffee mugs and spoons fly into her body and disappear. She walks through the dark and the man can only feel her vibrations, her negative space. Inside her, amongst the planets she's swallowed, a different version of the couple exists lying on a bed together in a deleterious universe. Their heads are giant tropical birds squawking at the tropical birds drinking blood from the birdbath outside. The light outside is florescent neon. The bird man fucks the bird woman with a cock the size of a human arm. They squawk and squawk, spewing glow-in-the-dark sweat from their pores.

In this house is a boy who has a face like an egg. Meaning: the boy was born without eyes or a mouth so his parents paint a face on him every morning. They draw a face on him, dress him, and take him to the park where he mostly sits on the grass feeling the wind on his skin. The boy sits in the grass picking the grass. He picks and picks at the same spot for hours until the spot is dirt. Just below the dirt the boy feels a small face. It is the face he is missing. He runs his hands along its features and the face laughs.

This house is the water pouring down the steps from the bathtub, the fish flapping around on the living room floor. It is your chest which is made of fish, pouring out fish covered in dust, the dust that is your chest. It is a sore you are picking at in the mirror, water rushing over your ankles, yelling at yourself in the living room where fish are spilling from you like cut nets opening on the deck of a boat. You're in the tub below the water, mouth open, picking out all the hooks.

I forgot to tell you about the sixteenth house. There's this thing covered with something like skin banging its head into the hardwood floor here, working against the oozy film about it, contorting and banging its head. The thing's father watches, pant-less. Where his cock should be is skin made to look like an open lotus. He flicks it over and over. He holds a baby as he does it. The baby is a little man pretending to be a baby. The little man is dreaming of a giant machine in the sky ferrying skin to the stars. There's a hole in the machine. Thin sheets of skin fall all over the world.

In this house you get a call. Something terrible has happened to someone you love though the person on the other line won't tell you who it is or what has happened. But you know something has happened. You hang up the phone and tremble. You spend the next hour looking at the ingredients on boxes in your kitchen, on the cosmetics in the bathroom. You look in the toilet and notice it is growing a single human tooth.

The house is the cuts on your knees, the red rubbed into your skin. It is the blonde hair that grows out of the ground and the ground that grows away from the earth. It is the bite marks on your breasts and the face you can still feel pressed against it. You give birth. You give birth over and over again. Your daughters lie about naked in the fields braiding the yellow hair that grows there. They tie each other down to ground with it, writhing in hair, laughing the same horrible laugh. The earth moans as someone fingers it. Your bruises open like blinds and you open your legs. The black eye of a new beast peers out.

You are in a house in the future. I am dead by now and know nothing about it. I don't know so many things you know. You, walking and talking, receiving messages, knowing new machines. I live here in this house in this past which is less than modest, dirty even. I drive my son this way and that. It is often too hard to look at his face. It is hard to speak and see something you love so much. Other than that, life is squalor. I go to work and pay bills. In tatters, I look to you and your glowing lights, your many contraptions. I button my shirt and think of things I'll never see. I button my shirt which has a hole in it I'll never learn to sew.

You are in a house in the future. You are looking out the window at the fake landscape. The fake landscape is a small room outside your window made to look like a horizon. The grass is plastic and foam. You are foam. The fake sun flickers outside the window and you cry little plastic pieces. You press your foam hand into your foam chest. It leaves a perfect imprint of your hand. You wait a long time for it to come back up.

You are in a house in the future. The future is a sad voice. It is singing a song and making it sound sadder than it is. The future is blue walls, blue houses, blue wind, blue everything. It is the people painted and without clothes, coming out of those houses, now looking at war ships in the sky. You know what color the war ships are. You know what color their bombs and bullets are too. What is surprising is the new shades of blue they make in the already blue sky. It deletes blue, recreates blue. Blue ash falls.

You are in a house in the future. You are looking out the window at the white lake. You are looking out the window in a white corridor which leads to another white corridor. There's a transmitter in your head which regulates color, sound, and taste. There is a man in a white booth filled with computers who controls the transmitter. He's turned your senses all the way down. You're barely a pulse. You're looking out the window at the white lake from the white corridor. There's a little black figure in a little black boat on the white lake. The figure rows but the boat doesn't move.

.

You are in a house in the future. You're in a long room where people in blue robes are scraping the skin off of people whose eyes are rolling back into their heads. You're the knives they are using. You feel everything. Skin floats to the floor like peels from an orange. There is in easel in front of each workers station that displays a charcoal drawing of a clock. Occasionally, the workers stop skinning to mark a new hour on the paper. The hours keep being invented one by one by one.

You are in a house in the future. You are watching a tiny television that has been surgically injected into your eye. You are standing with arms at your sides. You are slumped. Your finger twitches and the channel changes to a program where a man in a bear suit is standing alone in a cabin in the woods. The bear takes off his mask and it is you. You take off the bear paws and there are two small versions of your head where your hands should be. You bring them together and one bites the other and rips some flesh from its cheek. A woman you know walks in and rubs the belly of the bear costume and all the heads drool and moan.

You are in a house in the future. You have been exposed to gamma rays and a certain angle of weather that burns the eyes. You are acrylic and weekly, a man shining the shoes of a ghost in the subway, the ghost whose head is a metronome ticking back and forth and back again. The ghost shoves his hand into your brain and your brain is shoelace. It is the shoelace of every shoe you've ever owned unwound. He ties his finger around the lace you learned to tie with as kid. He makes bunny ears as a giant snail passes across the track where a train should be. There are wooden chairs with little arms and legs riding on the snail. They get off onto the platform and walk away holding umbrellas and newspapers and hats. It's all ridiculous no matter how you look at it: this coming and going, this tying, this great sigh.

You are in a house in the future. It is October in the future. There is man there wearing spoons and forks and knives all over his body and pointing at the silver-colored clouds. He is mumbling something to himself about setting the table. He is mumbling to himself about Christmas and the Sabbath and electrolytes. He passes a playground in what is otherwise blocks upon blocks of empty factories and crumbling grey bricks. The children playing on the playground have heads too big for their bodies. They run and their heads violently toss back and forth. You look down the street though the chain-link. There's a meter maid putting a ticket on a car whose face is a clean skull. You know for sure the skull is smiling. You know this for sure.

You are in a house in the future. You are weighing all the emotions in the house. You come up with different figures every few feet: 22 grams, 6 ounces, 15 pounds. You cup your hands in the air and watch the ceiling move like the throat of a toad. Outside the windows, men in hazard suits are testing the grass. The grass is making plans against you. Each blade bends to the other, whispering something low. The men in suits hold microphones against the ground. They play the recordings on speakers above a white van on the road so everyone in the neighborhood hears. Their yellow outfits blaze through the dark.

You are in a house in the future. You have just walked in to see your family after a long day at work. Your wife is a huge fork in a purple dress. Your daughter is a spittoon. The neighbors come into the house to spit into her and also spit into your face. You wipe away the spit from your face and look at your son. His head is a toaster with a stretched-out human face in the middle. You say: *son, there are some things in life you just have to accept.* Just then, a man then comes in, tightens his tie, and spits in your face again.

The house is the blue voice you move through, cars we spray-painted, a twenty year old pain in your chest that hasn't gone away. It is your plain name. It is your body sick of words, sick of the shapes that an s or a t or u can make. It is the words they piled into you in schools where you sat with kids cutting out their paper eyes, their paper tongues; words they gave you in hospitals that were as clean and sterile as the beds and the bathrooms and the tools that kept you still; words you learned in houses where you always keep the TV on mute, where you watch the colors the images make on the walls just to fall asleep. There are words for what you won't do, won't say. You leave the windows open in the house through its cold outside. You try to make out what is happening on the screen without looking at the TV. You hear the wind over everything which means you hear nothing. You're on the TV. There are little words below your skin trying to push themselves through. You poke at them with a piece of glass. You sit in the room and don't say a thing. A word scrapes itself out.

The house is a girl that won't wake up. It is the taste of blue pills dissolving on her tongue. It is the blue blanket on the bed flat where a body should be, a dream she's having forever. In the dream, the girl is the size of a human hand. She crawls under a door to feed the baby. The baby's head is too large for its body. It rolls back and forth and looks at the girl with its one black eye. The girl crawls into the baby's mouth and the baby chomps down on the girl. Her bones sound like the wind taking branches from the trees. Later, the baby cries and little versions of the girl roll down its face.

Each house is a thing I don't remember: a broken sea sliding over another broken sea, plastic and antibiotics, pink static and ugly slits. Each house is a thing I don't remember. You put your hands on the table and I shaped them like clay. I made your long fingers short and stout. I made your long fingers sharks and stars. I cut them up and roll them up and put them back together again. You said: *I like the way the cold feels on my hands and suddenly we were in a car.* There was nothing but white around us, white pines, white lights, white. You smoked and looked at me. Your pupils grew whiter and whiter. You were in the front seat then in the backseat, flickering on and off. We erased though I still heard the sound of the wheels over the road. Then there was no one in the car. Then the car was only scenery driving through different scenery. We were the radio turned on. We were only listening. I still can hear how we felt.

The house is having a dream. It's heartbroken. It's smelling the sheets, taking the loss deep into the chest. The sky is moving on how people do. You read a poem by an old woman that says colors are jewels. How indissoluble, the colors. And the body, too. *Not a jewel,* the house would say, *a stone.*

The house is the little clouds you put in the mirror. You move them with your giant hands. You talk about sad porch things, dumb things. You talk about my friend Paul. You eat the lowest piece of mirror you can find and it makes a sound like seeing things in your stomach. You hold out your hands and someone coughs. You've seen so many things. The seen things move back and forth in your head. One is a picture of you in a mirror in a drawer. The drawer is filled with blood. You love the sound it makes as it pours out.

The house is a street in a city I cannot remember. It is how I liked looking at each building, each storefront, knowing I would forget it. I walked into a gallery in this city and the paintings on the wall were of me in houses. Starlings covered the gallery floor, chirped loudly through the front doors of their mouths, chirped as they flitted out of our way, each step changing the landscape of their bodies in the room. I looked at the paintings in their frames. I thought about paint and wood, wood and paint, structure and light. I thought of the walls which break the air apart. I looked at myself, the tiny daps which made my face.

The house is the way you are trying to tell me to feel more. We are looking at the walls now because we have never seen anything else but walls together. We are looking at walls and thinking this could be the exact moment we fall in love, fall apart, fall out of the habit of living our lives. We look at the walls thinking of trees. The wall trees shake and it is lovely. It is the way you say lovely. It the way you say lovely which is lovelier than anything else.

In the seventieth house there are fifteen rooms that don't understand each other and ten that are content with what they are. There is a room for congruence and continuation and a room for the lilies to lilt, a room for the lilies to speak with the voices we are afraid to make, those strange voices that once took care of us in the dark. In the seventeenth house there are prayer hands and sad hands. There are hands that fold and never open; hands bruised for what they've touched and hands bruised for what they never found. In the seventieth house, every morning is a hard morning of women in plain clothes bracing the cold for someone else, sea birds frozen to the lake. Every morning is a man who does nothing for the ones he loves. He sits on the edge of the bed where the sun feigns to warm him. He puts his hands to his knees as if anything could hold him up.

The house is the vacant children and the medication we feed them. It is fences which delight the neighbors and the neighbors who stand visible in places, the neighbors who fill a construct, the neighbors who are long lines on numberless clocks. You watch the neighbor water the grass next door. His face is a wave that keeps crashing, ebbing, crashing. He waves and something in you dies for good. The plastic leg of a lawn chair bends below you. You like it.

In the house someone named *Faded Figure Pictures* follows you on Twitter. It makes you think of the drones in the sky. It makes you think of little paper men bent against a large grey wall panting their paper breathes, resting before fluttering away with the wind. You're the pictures a camera takes of itself, its own reflecting. You're a fake knife. You're a drunk text. You're the damage that doesn't know it's been done.

The house is a series of transgressions. It is the trunk of a car opened in a field, the soft sounds of shovels, headlights pouring through the long grass, a body slipped slack from the world. It is a boat floating on the sea whose crew has disappeared, a series of empty boats making a circle in the water like ribs for the body of the Earth. Eve's dream, maybe. And you're alone in the woods. No animals carved in the stars. No men or muses. You sleep and each day wake with less of yourself, less land to travel. Then one day, without warning, there are two of you.

The house is a beauty pageant for dead daughters. Their mothers bring their old dresses which they drag along the promenade. They hold white pieces of paper covered in too much makeup, too much rouge, too sexual. The papers make the fathers of the dead girls uncomfortable and sick to their stomachs. The papers make little kissy faces on the stage and the mothers in the dressing room wipe off the pages for the next segment. The pink wallpaper in the dressing room rips itself off the walls and collects into the shapes of little girls and large men hovering. The wallpaper looks at the mothers with its empty, flowery eyes. The mothers kiss the pages once more.

What the house is made of is of no consequence to you. You say *plaster* but mean *hunger*. Your say *nails* but mean *equity* and *time*. From August to May, the house is field noise before becoming the field meal in June. You and the family throw land and field where they should be. You call what's left to throw, house; a final bridge between vague greens and blues. When you're done, the family puts everything back where they think it should go, but the pieces of land and field and house don't quite connect. They bring back things. Every window looks at the same field from the same angle. You hear the sound of women combing their hair. There is a sense of being dizzy from having been so still.

The house tells you to change your life. It says *walk more.* It says *be better to yourself.* It says *flesh is an opening in a landscape of blood and didactics.* You sit in the sun so simple next to your abstractions. You stand up in the lawn for no reason. You stretch your arms in the air as if every word is not an ugly, horrible word.

The house is incarnate, worn over, mercurial. It fills with remorse the way a man does. Today the man is pretending to sleep on the living room couch so he can listen to his wife in the next room tell their son a story about a castle. "The wind sounds sad and lonely there," the wife says to the son. "Can the wind sound sad and lonely?" she asks. "No, only people," says the son. And the man tightens his eyes like the wind holding its breath.

The house suddenly happens. There is nothing to do about it but liken it to the ocean in that the word makes you think of anemia, black holes, criticisms, and all the things that happen to a body when it is emptied of itself. You say *ocean* but it doesn't replicate this feeling. It is only when the word is typed alone on a white page that you understand nothing better than you understand yourself. You are a little boy in headphones who grows up to become a clot, a faraway town, a plunging. In print: *ocean*. Because this is the nowhere you were meant to become. You stand at a kind of surge; a strong, meaningless tide. You part from the human shore.

YOU AND
OTHER PIECES

ONE

There's a village whose main inhabitant is the sound of distant gunfire. Hours float by like the shuffling of blank cards. Like an infant inside a bombed-out building playing with a bowl of oranges. Like this pier where two factory workers cast their lines from a boat. Because fishing is prayer. Is the catechism light makes with water and the bare, brown trees which surround it. Is the smokestack morning. Is waiting to see a blue curtain part in the window of a house where everyone is sleeping. Is a cook smelling his own hands after work. Too tired to eat. And with hands as worn as a cutting board. And with the scent of spices he's never owned still lingering in his hair.

~

What is a hallway flooded with light and silence in any building, at anytime, anywhere? Like here. Where the elevator shaft has been empty for years. Where the rows of doors make a sound. Make a sound like the violence that has a boy on a playground crying without ever opening his mouth. Like watching a cloud reach the end of the sky.

~

Who hears the bullet first? Is it the sniper or his mark? And is the sound like a pit bull barking at its master through chain link? Or like two lovers coming at the exact same time and only one of them is pretending. How the ragged cloth they've shared so many nights is starting to rip in half like a wishbone. How you remember standing in your kitchen as a kid. You're holding one end of the bone and your mother holds the other. You stare at each. Your eyes say the same thing. *I need this. I need this.*

~

Tell me about the color of my skin again. Paraphrase it. Then follow my scars like electrical wire. Come live in my neighborhood. Follow the width of my shoulders like the wingspan of an angel who's been stuffed and put on display in a museum of dead telephones. Tell me my history again. Show me something other than an empty flagpole. Lend me your accusation. Lead my hands to the ground. Lead my hands to the fabric that erases every face.

~

You call what opens the screen door a gust. Gust. How only we could make something so large sound so very, very small. Like calling what killed our family bullets. How we chalk up all the numbers and call them war.

~

Does a cloud ever reach the end of the sky? You've never seen it happen. Never stopped to take the time to watch.

How there's a girl standing on the wreckage of what was once a beach. Autumn. And there's not a cloud in the sky. Only a blue that's too dark to tell where the weather is going. And it's far too cold to be sitting out there, on drift-wood, while a war is going on. But you see her and know if you simply stopped to sit beside her there'd be nothing but the sea reaching out before you. Even further than where any cloud could ever go. But you keep on driving. You keep on driving with the image of her red hat blazing inside your skull. Red as if you'd just walked through the door after work and found blood on the carpet. But you keep on driving. You keep on driving. Cause there's a war going on…

TWO

There is a name for skin in the Republic. They call it *Mara*. Mara characterized as a shade so pale it sometimes glistens like porcelain and sometimes looks like a white crayon that's melted in the sun. Those born with Mara are often prone to erratic itching spells. But don't let the bandages fool you. The Mara wear bandages for no apparent reason. Maras noted as frequently hiding wounds that are not wounds.

~

You quickly learn to avoid the houses with blue lines painted on their front lawns. Fog rolls in. You look at the sky. Clouds float by with muscular precision like the tough thighs of horses.

~

Such bright colors in the cafes! The opposite of music happens. You feel the militias pour in. Kids on bicycles ride around the streets at night looking for unlocked cars. We're so poor we buy spray-paint for the spider webs. We make them decorations.

~

The man who sits in the field with a bare easel babbling to himself. He's naming the crows again. *Come here, Henry! Come here!* And the kiss noises he makes at them seem more hostile than soothing. A rapist's kiss.

~

They say "as is everything" instead of "it's always something" here. Is there a difference?

~

I cannot escape yellow. It's all over me. I see it even in the color of my own eyes. In the buildings. In the yellow dog barking at the yellow sky.

~

Almonds. I smell them in the trees, the rain, even through the glass. I don't have enough ingredients for soup so I just let the water boil all night. The gurgle of it becomes the ache in my temple. I run my finger into a sewing needle on the table. The window above the stove is so fogged I paint your picture in it. The marks of my hand. Dried blood. Steam and steam and steam.

~

Bent sails in the harbor. They all seem to want to touch the water. They all seem to hear what the water says.

~

The mud in the clearing is not quite red and not quite brown. Autumn. The woman who peels bark from the tree has no mouth or eyes. Just three black holes that seem to come together. Three holes as one hole. No nose.

~

The boys who steal birds' nests come along with small holes pecked in their hands. One comes wearing a nest like a hat. He's pulling off a scab with his teeth.

~

You always put your work shoes on the kitchen table. It reminds me that anything goes here. Leaves slowly float past the fronts of houses. People walk by without a word. Your neighbors never seem to eat the fish they catch. They hang a whole reel of them together. They spin in the wind like a baby's mobile. Scales and blank eyes. Blank eyes and scales.

~

This is your chair and this is my chair. My chair is the appeasing chair. It is far too hard and the cushion seems to sink inside itself. Your chair honestly makes me sick. Makes me gag. Look! Just listen! I'd do anything for you! Ask me! Tell me! Please! I swear it!

~

This tree is too high to be among the harvest. It's unholy. It needs cut down. Because the trees are too tall to be sick. All their language of *not say* is unbearable.

~

There's a nun peeling the skin from a yellow apple. Her hands are the roughest hands in the Republic. She reminds us of God. Getting to the meat of it. Skinning the gold from the sky.

~

Walk the circle of men. You'll see your future in your brother's shoulders. Your brother who is your enemy. Your brother who is you. You trade hearts. You trade tongues.

~

So many blistering red doorways to this world. So much dropping, dripping into. Red and fish tears. And all the while on stage a harlequin plays an old trombone.

~

The family bible is kept open but all I see inside it are pictures of empty cabinets, empty drawers. A cat yowls outside.

~

Physostegia, gladiolus, and lychnis. The rooftops look scared. They seem to sense the bomb which has yet to be invented and their shift among the elements. They grow tired of each other. They stand as still as lovers parting. Jesus, your eye is truly moving! It is traveling further up your forehead in the café as if it's following a fly. I watch it too.

~

You decided to make a go of it on foot. The image of things cut away from other images. It's as if you're drunk and shredding apart your least favorite paintings. You say the stills are comforting. You made plaster casts of your hands as if to remember what they could do, what they're for. When I asked you why you burned them you assured me they were not needed anymore.

~

Boats line the beach as if the ocean lost its child. As if the wind were its father who taught it to walk. Who split a path inside the wheat that lead it into the far too wild. Who disappeared. Ropes hanging from the dead ships clop against wood like the keys of a piano built without wires.

~

Let's sleep among the bales again! I'll carry your shoes. I'll make a thousand names for noon. Names that sound true.

~

I dropped the key in the piss pot so you couldn't leave. I hung your pants to dry by the fire. The fire that crackles like a kennel full of all the Republic's lost dogs. But what shall we do with this table? Where shall we put it? Who brought it to us?

~

I said I could do so much with a girl in white so you slapped me. She was so very plain and frail. I was afraid for us all.

~

Her infant is always trying to suck on the dirty curtain. I put it up on a hook. We cannot afford to take the curtains down.

~

There is a single lark floating above the wheat. It reminds me of the multitudes of v- patterned birds that came and went with the storm. V into v into V into v. The big and small flocks as systematic as bells. All of them moved eastward as the sky split into halves. One was bright yellow and one was bright black. The ground was gold. We passed an empty shop full of chairs and ladders. You sobbed because you had nothing to draw with. You truly sobbed.

~

The women mending nets. The weavers. The key. The milk. The willows like green angels spreading the many branches of their wings. The milk gone bad. The porch. Wind-bitten leaves. The broom carrying with it the dust. The milk even worse. The gathering of wood. The sting of lice. The young man in a cap. The postman. The head of a woman. Filling the pots with the flowers. The flowers die. We fill the pots with flowers. We smell the milk. Brothels. Cafés. Brothels. People pass over bridges. People stare at the bulbs. We drink the milk which is milk no more. Women wash in the canal. Ox and cart. Churches. We save money for more milk. We itch the lice. We struggle turning the key in the door. We break a branch from a green angel's wing. We throw our foul out the windows. We soil the brick. The brick reeks below us. The mess of brick makes us uneasy. We buy milk. We pass a girl with an orange. Coal barges. Cottages. Goats. Peasants and gypsies dancing. The key breaks in the lock. We get into the house through the window. Only the window. No doors. Two figures stroll down a country lane. Two figures like parallel lines down tracks. They never cross. Parallel lines. Couples hold each other. A crab falls on its back and cannot move. Its claws open and close but it cannot move. The milk goes bad. Red cows fill the field. The many socialites blend together in their halls like a beast with many heads. We smell the milk. A peacock moth with my face inside it. My face in thin colors that live. The drinkers by the docks in their top hats gulping slosh into the thick fuzz of their bellies. Henry comes. The crow who swallows a whole dove whole. He fills the black of him. We pass the dunes. We take off our wet socks. The rain blends into the field. We drink the milk which is milk no more.

~

How is it that the man who left his family is less crazy than you? How he wields his yellow sword.

~

The dead watch him. The nude browns. His life. How he wanted so much more. Your bare back shining as fresh water runs down it. So slow. So slow.

~

After the sermon the green angels locked horns. Yellow light fell through their branches as we cupped our hands together. We were that much closer to the silence we could never reach. We looked inside the spaces of our fingers as if the dark we'd caught could shine.

~

Are you jealous of him? He carves the wood as he knows you crave the sound of the knife. He lets you rub the dust off the floor. And when he goes he'll leave the blade…

~

You handed me something wrapped in paper and begged me to keep it. A slug the peasant children covered with salt. The broken end of a brush. A lost shell.

~

And now I know you've reached your end. The sow. The fields of wheat. This dark green so quiet below the clouded sky. So ominous. Like the crows. The chips of paint peeled away. The spirals you found in everything. The bullet the doctor wouldn't take out. The sketch he made of you. How I tried to think hard of you wrapped in the red blossoms falling from the tree. Tried to think of you believing the stars you saw in the sky were like the lanterns they'd hang from the heads of horses. Tried to think of you escaping all the yellow halls and embittered cafés. The missing parts. The women all so pregnant with loneliness and too old for their fancy hats. The unsympathetic cousins. The hands of loves ripping through dirt. The yellow flowers. The reworked impressions. The galleries and galleries unneeded. How the willows finally lifted you from the earth.

~

And I often think of the first day you came to the Republic. You said you were a painter…

THREE

A line has been made between us and our enemy. The earth it dug poured open with green light, with a rumor of new rain, a hive of sound. Who were you then but a bridge falling? A rhapsody of branches before your voice, smelling of almonds, whispering? A mistake a musician made on his final recording. A finger stuck to the string for a moment too long. What now with this hammer and smash of us? This red imprint of my hand glowing on her skin like a lit bulb? And her dark hair. Her dark hair wrung around my fingers like the blue strings of a marionette. How is it that it holds me still? With strings. With missed messages on the machine. With strings that make no music at all.

~

There are men in this world who insist that the rubble of their village smells sweet. Sweet. How it seemed everything there hung from a leather strap. Women in shawls and hijabs walked past bullet-ridden, tiled walls and smelled only of sweat. Green tile followed them everywhere. The kind you find inside of old bathrooms in parks. Something churned in the air. Some kind of wild chanting. A malnourished boy with a fly embedded in his head was carrying the weight of his ribs. He was trying to pick himself up with his elbows. There was an explosion. I watched the boy open. The boy was made of flies.

~

Women were forced to marry men deformed in battle. Men without faces, hands, or cocks. They stood beside each other unnaturally. I remember a bed I shared with one of them. She told me her husband's skin still smelled like a campfire. She told me how clean his white suits were.

~

There were bullet holes in all the windows. I couldn't believe how real the world looked through the holes. How much faith we'd put into glass. I accidentally shot my reflection out of a mirror a few yards away. Shots responded to my mistake. More glass shattered. Children with guns and machetes stormed the gates.

~

Fields spread out below the aircrafts in strange squares. Like wallpaper slowly dissolving off of the walls in a room you couldn't even imagine. Different shades of green and brown in variation. How do we do that to the earth? Divide it into strips like that. How some of what's plowed comes up chalk-white. The way a man is sometimes framed into the ground by a bomb blast. How where we landed was charred black but these bursts of paper were floating in the air everywhere. Tattered about from an office that was no longer standing. Pieces of it pressed hard by the wind into stone.

~

There were women sobbing together in doorways. Of all age and description. We began pushing them aside to pull bodies out of the basements of tenements. Fights broke out. A woman pulled one of our men's jaws so hard by the teeth that it broke in the struggle. She was ushered away with gunfire. Like target practice. The bullets seemed to carry her away forever. Like a cowboy at the end of a movie who is riding into the sunset. And the bodies on the truck never made their destination. A roadside bomb. How they seemed driven into the sunset too. How later a tree that wasn't even close to the blast toppled over without explanation.

~

There were misgivings from the start. The heat was unbearable. Our supplies were nearly gone. We'd found ourselves crawling through the poppy on our stomachs and I remember longing for wheat. For rye. I was so exhausted I fell asleep in the mud and dreamt men in ski-masks were throwing Molotov cocktails at a cherry blossom tree. The one you'd had tattooed on your arm. And there were these wax figures of famous people spread all over the beach. Some bobbed back and forth in tide. An old, famous actress was propped on a piece of driftwood but pieces of her face were melting away from the heat of the tree. But then the screaming woke me. They were crawling through the poppy with us. A line had been drawn.

FOUR

There are men in the Republic who lose every cent of their relief fund on cards. They're like the dead who never stop bleeding. Who float like the drowned rats of the canal inside their own caskets. Scarecrows that the blackbirds live inside. Who make their way home past church gates like floating mirrors. Who find that the empty plates that greet them on the kitchen table reflect them perfectly. And their families are afraid to say their name. To wake them. They're more like a dream about the man who was their father that is always happening. But sometimes he cracks a smile. Sometimes he plays music for no apparent reason. A girl counts coins with a man posing as her father. They smile at each other.

~

We woke to men shooting their hunting rifles up at the sky. They were standing in the square. Their wives stood beside them shielding their eyes from the sun.

~

I saw your blue bike leaned against the side of the tavern but decided not to go in. There was an old ambulance sounding off near the camp beyond the woods. And I think of all the refugee girls who escaped the camp only to sell their bodies out of the motels. Motel Street. The bull rings they set up. How they might be the only ones who are making a profit out of this war. And I feel so tired. I almost steal your bike to pedal myself home.

~

There were men being pulled from machines with teeth painted on them. Men in small bunkers surrounded by sandbags. People in white aprons and surgical masks seemed to constantly enter and exit without saying a word. Women in fatigues leaned against a tank smiling for a camera. How plain they were to the men on their knees. Men who pray in makeshift tents because every church has been bombed for miles. Men who'd learned to live wherever they found themselves. Men who'd become more an element like rain. Wet clothing covered every branch. And when they slept they breathed the way that rain suddenly comes. Their breathing deepened everything. Sunk everything. Like black smoke that billows forever. Like an inflatable craft that finds itself before a gunship. Political rallies of men maddened with idealism. With the symbols and propaganda that create a God with the sole purpose of destroying another. That burn effigies. Hang effigies. Rip effigies apart with wild hands in mass crowds. Crowds who've gathered simply to destroy their own small part of an effigy. Like violent pioneers seeking a patch of land on a new continent. Men who've grown tired of all this. Men who will settle for effigies no more.

~

Two soldiers lay dead together in the road. You immediately mistake them as lovers in bed. How they'd been stripped of everything but their pants. Their helmets like turtles some kids had flipped onto their backs.

~

There is always dust on the sergeants' coats. They line the fences of the refugee camp trading cigarettes for information. They ignore the men tied to pipes by a brick building with bandanas covering their faces. They ignore a human hand which juts out like a white flag from a heap of trash. A mandolin is playing from a tent. One of the sergeants grabs a refugee by the collar through the fence. A single blast blows through the back of the refugee's head. He falls limp on his knees. His head leaned against the fence. Hands behind him. Things go on without missing a beat. The music continues. Deals are made. Dogs bark.

~

You'd gone into a building looking for food and found a man who'd been burned alive while sitting on a chair at a table. Do the dead really sit? Yes. How the burns made him look like he had a dark fur covering his body. You walked out into the sun and ate the crackers. They were horribly stale. Almost tasteless. They got you through another day.

~

There was one Christmas we wrapped the food we'd stolen from the veteran's hospital and gave it to the children as gifts. You'd combed your hair. Your brush had seemed long forgotten. Just a toy in the baby's crib.

~

Statues are toppled to the ground. Yesterday's currency becomes today's souvenir. Why save anything? These men seem to be born without knowing why. They die the same way.

~

They'd hung pro-war pictures at the men's club in the Republic. Old men in navy suits clop about telling bad jokes and smoking cigars. They had fifteen cakes made to celebrate the anniversary of something that had little or no significance to anyone in the world but the club. An old man with a cleft lip and a fez came by and slapped me on my back. I stared at their heroes on the wall. Their sons. Their grandsons. Their lives reenacted by death. By memorial.

~

There were bags full of leaves all over your lawn. Pieces of your blue bike were placed on rags in front of the garage. A fire was burning out back and only a few leaves remained on the utmost tips of the trees. They looked like lit matches. A beautiful day. And I didn't know what had brought me to you. Some coffee? Some conversation? Social workers were pounding on your neighbor's door like they do every Sunday. Kids in the road were yelling a name at me that wasn't my name. Our little joke. And I was knocking on your door. I was trying to figure out what brought me to you when you opened the door. We'd lost so many years. We'd shared little more than a common language. But there was that. And that was everything.

FIVE

Remove magazine. Use charging handle to pull bolt to rear. Lock it by opening the hold. Pull charge handle to rear and release the hold open. Let on the forward. Take the cross pin and press it. This will release the hold and let the bolt move forward. *How the body can be opened by a machine.* Press out the cross pin. Make sure to tip the upper receiver so the bolt can be removed. Remove changing handle. *This clattering of gun parts on concrete. You like the competition of sound the pieces make. MP magazine.* Ammo holder. *And you wish there was a way to assemble the body. To dissemble it cleanly.* Front sight. Rear sight. Business side. Backside. An empty bolt in the AR-15. Close the bolt. *The butt stock in the face. The mashed teeth.* And I take the action out. Take it from fire to safe. Push the pin. Take the upper from the lower. The charging handle. The forward assist. *There were men in gas masks at a check point. It looked like they were breathing fire onto the windshield of the truck.* Reduce the recoil. AA-12. M107. Ten rounds in ten seconds. Handle the recoil. For your .50 AE use a rebated cartridge. Notice the reduced kick. Muzzle blast and flash. Field strip the pistol. The magazine is improperly seated. Run the brush through the chamber till it reaches the other end. *A refugee woman in the front seat was screaming. Her window was open so the fire waved in and singed her hair. Her face was melting off the bone. She was trying to drive in reverse but it looked like her left hand had become a part of the steering wheel.* Oil the chamber and bore with a patch. Clean glass cylinder. *The glass in the car was evaporating.* Remove deposits from the glass cylinder. *The soldier sitting shotgun shot himself through the mouth.* Oil all the other parts and reassemble. *It seemed like those red spots would stay in the air forever. Like time stopped. But I heard the growl of the fire come over the truck again. I had to trample over a soldier just to smash out of the back window of the car. His glasses were red. I wasn't sure whose blood was whose.*

~

For a while I wore a bandage around my hand. I remember there was an afternoon she washed me in a bathtub like a child. Her child. The scar we found below all that dirty wrapping looked like an *L*. It was her scar. Her pink-red initials punctuated by tiny, thread-like dots. Her map that always brought me back to the same place. To a bare light morning where we both laid in bed trying to sleep. How the pain finally set in. How the space between us below old sheets numbed out the sound of the birds. And it was like being born a new thing. A wounded thing. A hurt thing she had made so new. So new it barely knew where to lay its hand. Or how to sleep. And it had to learn. It had to learn how to sleep again.

~

Check points were the same. Papers. You'd be taken out of a car and searched of everything. Roadblocks. Stoplights. Taxi drivers were always suspect. How some of the stops kept souvenirs. They'd nail body parts of suspected revolutionaries to the sides of buildings. Hands. Ears. Legs. Illuminated under checkpoint lights against yellow, bloodstained walls. Like slaughterhouse pigs. How at one stop a guard had brought his children with him. They were on the roof of a checkpoint building. They were waving down at us. We were waving back.

~

You'd get nervous and make mistakes. A glance would happen. A glance that meant the end of the world. Water-boarding. Choking and coughing for years in small brick rooms without lights. So suddenly there's the sound of a grenade rolling into a doorway. Yelling and a few shots. And you never knew who was more surprised. You never know if the ache in your stomach was right. You'd hear the sound right before the explosion. The last clack. And you'd say yes to yourself. *Yes. Yes.*

~

There's always a child crying on this street. That is how we tell the children apart. By their cry. And the cat is peering into the cage where we'd put a mouse for your daughter. It sits there all day without moving. Without begging. Just pawing at the bars. And it's our baby crying now. The baby is pulling stuff off of the shelves. Pulling down jars from cupboards without doors. And finally we hear the cage tumble down to the floor. We wonder how it took this long.

SIX

There are men who bring news of the dead. They were
recruiters before the draft. They were murderers before
they were messengers. Our dreary archangels. We avoid
them on the streets. We spit at them from project bal-
conies. With their boxes of dead flags. As useless as an
altar of birds on a swing in a childless village. As useless
as a pile of skulls. With their papers always needing to
be signed. With documents hanging from a staple like a
scythe. *Azrael.* The angels who walk among us. All the de-
scendants of Azrael. We see in their faces the true mean-
ing of angels. To make more angels.

~

They put hoods on the nude prisoners. They're lined
against the wall waiting for instructions. Even longing
turned against them now. How a bone becomes disjoint-
ed. Fragmented. How even desire is interrogated. Like
meaning in a psalm. How they're piled on top of each
other in a pyramid. How they try protecting each other's
genitals from a frothing dog. Jerked and blown by each
other. Indistinguishable from each other. Exploited. Un-
til their bodies are one body in the dark. Until even love
becomes their enemy's face.

~

Call them angels. Boots smashing into a baby's crib. Raping a young boy. Slitting the throat of a woman on the front stoop. As it happened she must have been remembering something. How she wrote the name of this city on her wall as a child. How she promised herself she'd get here. When the war began she remembered saying every culture laughs to her son. She was thinking of her wedding day. How tears came as easily as money. She was thinking of the name of that city written on her bedroom wall.

~

There must be some evidence somewhere. How September was an angel falling. An angel hidden below unending debris. An angel who burned all the way down like a cigarette in the hands of a man who knows he's dying. How the skyscraper morning caught everything in its onslaught of windows. Caught the coil of building which tumbled like a freight train from the sky. Caught the white van parked on the sidewalk with cameras ready. And it occurred to you then that there was only one difference between your God and their God. Their God's wrath was accounted for. Their God kept a body count. *Pull it.* That's what your God said. *Pull it.* And you stood all day in the yard. You were amazed there wasn't a single plane left in the sky.

~

You remember when it was your job to watch the banquets of food that were set for the soldiers' parties. The refugee kids would show up out of nowhere from the hills. Their eyes seemed to gather it all in. To eat every morsel with watery looks. And suddenly you knew what it was like. To be the one without pity. To be the one who had to say no.

~

You hear reports of a man who was dragged out of subway car by an angel in broad daylight. You hear this and dread the end of every bottle. You dread the pinhole that exists between the end of every night and every day. You dread crossed fingers. You dread the smell of her on your cock. Your mouth. Even the tips of your nails. Dread the unhinging of what your arms do. Dread the word *fortitude. Patience.* Because when you tell me I don't have to justify myself I cannot be myself. I cannot be anyone who doesn't need justification. Without sin. Because I am undressing you idly. I am slinking my hand down the curve of your thigh. I am pulling your hair and fucking you till you cry. Because I want pain from love. Not mine. Yours. Your pain. Because the slow unbuttoning, the careful exposure of your shoulder, is nothing but you, nothing but what I have. Like all the wings hidden below trench coats. Below age and passports and beards. As if everything that lives forever must remain beautiful. Perfect. Untouched. Justified.

SEVEN

There is a cellist still sitting in the orchestra pit of a the-
ater after the rehearsal. Silhouettes talk behind dark red
curtains in code. Codes changed every Friday. Workmen
smoke and sweep through rows of red, velvet chairs. She
cannot move. She's dreaming of how the male cellist's
worn hand had played the harp of her ribs below her
blouse. His hand on her bare back. How it made her
heart feel like a prisoner whose mouth had been taped
shut. Her heart a black telephone always ringing in a
black city where men have memorized all of her con-
versations. Her heart a church being pulled apart down
the road. Doors and pews strewn around the courtyard.
Covered with snow. Covered with birds who could pick
the whole world clean. Her heart an angel who greets the
earth facedown. Drowned on all of space. Her heart a
bridge we sleep below. A woman's heart. Simply a wom-
an's heart whose ribs you can feel so plainly but who is
anything but starving. Is starving. Her heart how slums
face one another. Her heart a long line of Christmas
lights that cannot be unwound. A rooftop full of all the
children's lost balls.

~

A horn player drinks coffee by his window in the Republic. He watches a girl in a pink dress play through the fog. Only barely. He can barely see anything but a few roof-tops here and there. Blackened by rain. Rooftops and the girl's pink dress by railroad tracks. She's writing a boy's name on the sole of her shoe. His wife appears on the stoop carrying groceries. He looks at the fresh bandages on her arms. Her black eye. He looks and wonders if she can see him behind the glass. He turns away. The whole house smells of lentils. A gray cat paws at his leg. He picks it up and tosses it across the hardwood floor without looking where it lands. He's amazed by the shadows in the house. How large they are. The door opening.

~

They're sitting around a table in an apartment forging papers for refugees in the camps. They're used to talking without speaking. They almost prefer it. They work in silence as snow falls. A bassoon player sits in a green chair by a fire. He's holding a bomb wrapped in a newspaper. He can hear a few men arguing in the bedroom. Harsh whispering. A bottle is thrown at someone's face. Louder whispers. Parts are spread all over a bare mattress that's black from dirt. Two pale children watch the argument from the couch. Both of their mouths are taped shut. Gray tape. And suddenly they all stop working. They're afraid to move. A woman passes by in the hallway to let her dogs out. She's singing to herself.

~

Two men in black coats watch the conductor from a crack

in a hotel door. He's noticed but doesn't care. He's grown tired of it all and is more upset about the lighting in the hotel. The lobby is too bright. The floral arrangements. The wallpaper. Too bright! Everything is too bright! He sits in the bathtub covered in sheet music. Head bobbing to the music he's imagining the way a man deafened in the war remembers a voice he'd once heard. How he cannot remember who it belonged to. He closes his eyes. Thinking. He sees it! Almost. Almost.

~

That was the wrong alley. The wrong way home. And the flute player is tied to the radiator. Her wrists burn against them. But another man is coming inside her. There are twenty of them. And another is coming. And another. And another. And they don't open the window when they hang her from a bed sheet. The radiator makes a creaking sound. Glass falls on the road.

~

The viola player is amazed by her skin. She's standing in a butcher shop. Butchers are chopping apart a pig. Its pink ears flap back and forth on a wooden block like huge wings of an airplane that could never fly. Chicken heads are on the floor. Blood on the tables like syllables we have yet to use or find. The butchers yell at each other in a language she cannot understand. She's amazed by her skin. Amazed how it covers her body. How it feels everything. Everything. And when it opens, when it tears, it covers itself again. Heals. Blisters. Scars.

~

There are endings everywhere. We write elegies for the living. And a clarinet player believes his wife is hiding inside the belly of a statue in the Republic. A black angel riding a horse. He remembers how his wife would laugh at it. *Why does an angel need a horse?* He thinks she must know now. That maybe its wings had been broken. Burned. She must know the story now. Must know why angels ride horses on earth. Why they've chosen to look like men. Women. Why they wield swords. So he reads a book on a bench. He's asking the book questions he's long since known the answers to. He's biding his time. He's waiting for the angel to give birth. He's waiting for more statues to sit beside.

~

Animals who cannot turn around cannot be trusted, the oboe player says. He's become obsessed with backwards. He dreams his wife walks backwards after a car moving backwards on the wrong side of the road. How she seems to be pulled away from him in every picture he owns. And he dreams of rain returning to the sky. Factories taking back their guns. Flowers being sucked back into the earth. He cannot stop it from happening. *We're being sucked into a big hole,* he says. Us. Our histories. A hole. And he's having trouble breathing. He collapses in the yard where he's raking leaves. It occurs to him. He's the hole. The leaves float across the yard to him like magnets. Like worms to a casket. For hours. Nothing but leaves. They cover him.

174

~

The trombonist remembers the word *weekend*. He remembers what that meant as sails move past him in the channel. Like giant white words without meaning. Words that tread water. Like small talk at reunions no one wanted to go to. Like goodbyes to strangers. *Weekend.* Who knew the days would weld together? Would fugue themselves with the sky? Until everything was gray. Was brittle. Was as open and clear as water. And just as deep. Just deep enough to drown in. Though he's known men, even soldiers, who've drowned on less than what he has already drank that day. So what keeps the ocean from taking us in its arms? To dance us weightless and lifeless? What keeps the rain from carrying us like restraints or chains to the very center of the largest ocean and dropping us in? Body upon body. Floating on bodies. Then floated upon. What keeps us from drowning on the ocean inside? On each other? Water stretches behind him. A body of water that would take a lifetime to swim. Though it only takes a moment for the body to drown. You've known men who went out wading in the water. Who went out wading and kept walking. Who didn't return. The way angels must float past heaven. Past space. To something beyond what we call the universe. What we call eternity. To something beyond God's reach. Beyond his doctrines. His holy word. Even his invention. To where all angels strive to go. Call it nowhere maybe. Nowhere. Or beyond it.

~

There is a sudden bomb blast in the market. The tuba player first notices the pieces of fruit scattered about. Skin and pulp. The splintered stands. Screaming. He is eye-level with road. Ribboned about. Jigsawed about. Only a moment ago he'd been carrying around an instrument that had seemed too burdening. So heavy and large. His legs gone. His hand hanging from his wrist. Confetti. A piñata. He had not realized his body was an instrument that played itself. An instrument that was hard to carry. To contain.

~

The male cellist had begun the affair with faith. Without shame. He'd trusted her the way a child trusts the bright, red berries that grow on a bush in the yard. Or the warm mouth of a strange but healthy-looking dog. He'd begun it with music. He'd written her songs. Was sure that a song would come from that night. The moon over the water. How they'd walked so long in the woods. In the dark. He'd thought some music would come of this. But he's alone now in the house. The clock chimes at the same time. Without reason. His heart.

~

The bassoonist was the last to hear the concert had been cancelled. He lay dead on the steps of the theatre. His head opened by a single shot. The bomb below him wrapped in newspaper detonated under the force of his fallen body. The entrance of the theater evaporated in symphony. It woke the cellist who'd fallen asleep in her chair. Her hand holding her ribs. Her ribs holding her heart. It was Friday. She saw what looked like the wings silhouetted behind the red curtains. Stretching. She heard murmuring somewhere out in the empty theatre. Prayers that were not prayers. Codes had been changed.

~

There's a train stopped to be searched. People scatter about on row upon row of railroad. Hooded men sit on a rail. They're shot in order. People shout and swear and cheer from the warm light of a dining car. Dawn. Everyone outside the train seems to tremble. Silent. Smoking. Drinking. Like lost moths. Like pilgrims who'd just discovered that the world had ended. That there was no more of it to be found. But who's to say that's true? Who's to say there isn't a place for us? Place enough for a world of our own inside this one? Who knows? Two violinists stand on the back of the train. They play. Red leaves seem to mimic the music and the music seems to mimic us. Mimic what we cannot say about what our lives have become. Amounted to. Only that this is not where we wanted to be. That this was not the world we were promised. And the violins cut through the space between every branch. Every edge of every cloud. And everything aches with knowledge of itself. With the music that rouses its ache. Day in and day out: rouses it to live, to suffer, to survive.

ACKNOWLEDGMENTS

Pieces from this book have appeared in *The Kenyon Review,* *PANK, Caketrain, Better, Hobart, Make, elimae, Red Lightbulbs, Mudluscious Press, Keyhole Magazine, Gigantic*, and *MTV Books.*

Thanks to Michael J. Seidlinger for publishing this book and to Nicolle Elizabeth for her edits. Thanks to Nadxi Nieto for her cover design and to Pierre Schmidt for allowing us to use his artwork. Thanks to Brian Evenson, Gary Lutz, Peter Markus, and Cole Swensen for blurbs.

Thanks to Christopher Kennedy and Sarah Blake Schoenholtz for their help with *The House Is a Place Where Things Can Go Wrong*.

Thanks to my friends and family for their love and support.

And finally, thanks to you.

OFFICIAL

CCM ◖

GET OUT OF JAIL
* VOUCHER *

- -

Tear this out.
Skip that social event.
It's okay.
You don't have to go if you don't want to. Pick up
the book you just bought. Open to the first page.
You'll thank us by the third paragraph.

If friends ask why you were a no-show, show them
this voucher.
You'll be fine.

- -

We're coping.

◖